D1784667

CHRISTIANS
REMEMBER
YOUR
PAST LIVES
LEARN HOW

DOUGLAS CASIMIRI

authorHOUSE®

AuthorHouse™
1663 Liberty Drive
Bloomington, IN 47403
www.authorhouse.com
Phone: 1-800-839-8640

© *2013 Douglas Casimiri. All rights reserved.*

No part of this book may be reproduced, stored in a retrieval system, or transmitted by any means without the written permission of the author.

Published by AuthorHouse 7/19/2013

ISBN: 978-1-4918-0021-8 (sc)
ISBN: 978-1-4918-0020-1 (hc)
ISBN: 978-1-4918-0019-5 (e)

Library of Congress Control Number: 2013913108

Any people depicted in stock imagery provided by Thinkstock are models, and such images are being used for illustrative purposes only. Certain stock imagery © Thinkstock.

Because of the dynamic nature of the Internet, any web addresses or links contained in this book may have changed since publication and may no longer be valid. The views expressed in this work are solely those of the author and do not necessarily reflect the views of the publisher, and the publisher hereby disclaims any responsibility for them.

TABLE OF CONTENTS

PREFACE

Past-life regression is essential for improving the quality of your present life. This is especially true for Christians, as it will allow them to fully realize the teachings of Jesus and his beliefs about life and death.

The techniques you learn in this course will allow you to investigate far memory and determine for yourself how important this information is to your present life.

Most therapists already know the value of age and past-life regression. In many cases, past actions may have created current undesirable situations that you or someone else may find yourselves in today.

There is an awakening among people as they start to realize that we are much more than just physical beings who live for a brief moment in time.

We are the sum total of all our lifetimes, and our present life has been greatly influenced by memories of our previous lives. Our life today is the consequence of all the thought, action, and the choices we have made since our soul's creation. Our past-life memories contain our soul's history, and these memories are ready to be explored!

In my opinion, past-life regression may become the new therapy of the future. Regression therapy is finally becoming accepted by mainstream therapists as an extremely useful therapeutic process. It can be a quick tool for bringing issues to the surface in a single or just a few sessions. Many fears, phobias, and addictions that we are dealing with today may not have been created in this lifetime at all. The answers may lie in the past. Whether you believe in reincarnation or not, everyone has past-life memories.

In simple, easy-to-understand terms, this book will guide you through the process of becoming a Certified Past-Life Regression Facilitator, with no college degree needed. Whether your interest is just for fun, for self-improvement, or to develop your own practice or new career, this book will show you how to meet your goal step-by-step.

Now is the time to become involved in this fascinating area of human exploration.

CHAPTER 1

Introduction to Reincarnation

As I was watching television with my youngest daughter, we saw a scene where people were trying to get into a lifeboat. Out of the blue, my daughter said to me, "I was in one of those boats before." I sat there in astonishment. Then I calmly said, "Oh, yeah? Tell me about it."

My daughter went on to tell me that she and her daddy had been in a big boat that started to sink. Everyone was scared and yelling. Her daddy had picked her up and carried her to the little lifeboat. Her dress had gotten caught on the side of the boat, and he'd had to rip it to get it free. She had been upset that her dress had been damaged.

By then she had my attention. I asked her what her daddy looked like, and she said he had black hair and a big beard. I asked her what her name was, and she said it was Victoria. I went on with some more questioning, but she had been very young at the time of the boating incident and couldn't recall dates or last names.

This experience made me realize how natural it is for a person to recall past memories when they are properly instructed.

A past-life regression facilitator may come across many specific terms in this field of service. Before we discuss the facilitating process, let's define some of those terms and answer a few philosophical questions about reincarnation and past lives.

What Is Reincarnation?

I don't think anyone really knows for sure. What we do know is that our awareness and memories survive death, and we are reborn into new physical lives. Our souls, which never really die, pass from one body to another. We just change our physical form, forgetting who we once were.

Why Do We Keep Moving from One Lifetime to Another?

My best guess would be that our souls are striving for perfection, and most of us are totally unaware of this process. Those who are not connected to their spiritual side seem to identify primarily with the physical body. The fact is that our true nature is energy and spirit. Under a microscope, we see millions of particles, and all of them know where they are going and what they have to do. At that level, our bodies are nothing more than pure energy, and we know that energy never dies.

As far as we can see, our souls are forever growing and evolving, without beginning or end. Our individual souls have lived through lifetime after lifetime. We know this is a fact because we have memories from other times and places but don't know where they came from. There are thousands of well-documented past-life experiences. A lot of these past-life regressions have been facilitated by experts in many fields that study the human mind.

Another subject I find really fascinating is the area of pre-birth memories and communication. There are well-documented cases of this phenomenon and websites you can visit. In this situation, people recall existing in a spiritual plane before their births on earth. They often describe a spiritual existence that is very similar to the existence reported in near-death experiences. Not only do people with pre-birth memories describe a spiritual preexistence, but they also remember choosing their own parents and the types of challenges they will face on earth. Many of them recall seeing souls assembled together, waiting to be born again on earth. This offers further proof that we have lived before.

Through all the research that has been done, we know that every decision we have made in our past lives—and especially the decisions we are making in the present—are vital to our soul's journey. Our soul or spirit knows what it needs to evolve for its highest good. The soul wants to become whole and balance its energy. It must experience the effects that it has caused.

Although most of us may not always follow it, our own intuition is our soul's way of trying, based on its years of existence, to guide us along our path. Once we do start to follow our intuition, we will notice how many people, situations, and synchronicities start to appear, helping us along with our own personal journeys.

So, try to slow down, listen, and acknowledge your soul's wisdom. This guidance is there for you to tap into at any time.

A Brief History of Reincarnation

Reincarnation was discovered by accident. It started with various experiments with hypnosis. Early in the nineteenth century, in certain cases, a hypnotized person might have acted as if he was someone else. Sometimes the person spoke a different language from another place and time.

At the time, scientists had rejected the idea that the soul survives death. They called these memories "hypnotic hallucinations." It wasn't until the 1850s that the study of these hypnotic hallucinations started to be taken seriously.

Galitzin (1794–1866), a Russian prince and cellist who inspired Beethoven to write his last string quartets, performed a hypnotic experiment in 1862 with an uneducated German woman from Bad Homburg, who knew not a word of French. The observers were shocked when she began to speak fluent French.

The woman told a story about having lived before the eighteenth century, when she had been a countess in an Italian castle and had murdered her husband under circumstances that had appeared to be accidental. Therefore, her soul had had to return to live a hard life.

Galitzin later went to the place where the woman said she had lived, and he confirmed the historical existence of that particular countess.

This was a case of accidental regression, as it hadn't been the hypnotist's intention to take the person back in time.

The first intentional regressions seem to have been those of Jose Maria Fernandez Colavida (1819–1888) in Spain, a member of *La Paz*, a spiritist group in Madrid.

Esteva Espanola later reported about this phenomenon at a spiritist conference in Paris in 1900, after performing many regressions herself.

Another pioneer in this field was French spiritist Lieutenant Colonel Albert de Rochas d'Aiglun (1837–1914). He performed a number of these past-life regressions and published the first book on the subject, *Les Vies Successive.*

Sigmund Freud, during a phase in his life, also performed regressions—not to past lives but to a traumatic experience in the actual life of a patient who had suppressed the memory. Freud later left regression and developed his own form of psychoanalysis by means of free association.

Professor of psychology Theodore Flournoy (a teacher of Carl Jung) studied a spectacular case of Mrs. Helene Smith, who told of past lives while being regressed. Professor Flournoy called the phenomenon *cryptomnesia.*

Roy Martin, a teacher in Sharon, Pennsylvania, performed many regressions from around 1928 to the 1940s. He wrote a little-known book about his work called *Researches in Reincarnation and Beyond* (1942).

The British psychiatrist Alexander Cannon performed over 1,400 past-life regressions. He also wrote a book about his work called *The Power of Karma* (1936). The book was republished as *The Shadow of Destiny* (Kerringer and Whitefish 2005).

Another pioneer was the Swedish psychiatrist John Bjorkhem (1910–1963). He wrote a doctoral thesis entitled *De Hypnotiska Hallucinationerna* (1942). He reported a number of regressions where people went to different times and places.

Klein regressed a number of people in 1952, which is mentioned in *The Effect of Suggestion on Past-Life Regression*.

In 1956 a book was published by Henry Blyth: *The Three Lives of Naomi Henry*. Two of the past lives described therein were researched and confirmed.

Here is a brief list of some famous and influential individuals who have held a belief in reincarnation.

- Plato believed that the soul is older than the body and is reborn continuously into this life.

- William Wordsworth said "that our birth is but sleep and a forgetting. The soul that rises with us, our life's star, hath had elsewhere its setting. And cometh from afar."

- Kahlil Gibran said, "A little while, a moment of rest upon the wind, and another woman shall bear me."

- The ancient mathematician Pythagoras claimed to have remembered his reincarnations.

- Plotinus, in *The Descent of the Soul*, claimed to have knowledge of the soul and its origin.

- Salvador Dali claimed to vividly remember his past life as Saint John of the Cross.

- General Patton, on the plains in Europe, said, "I have been here before. I remember the battle."

These are just a few of the pioneers in this field, as there are too many to mention here. Since the 1960s, there has been a major increase in the number of regressions being performed. It has been proven that a regression can have a therapeutic effect, which has led to the establishment of what is now called "past-life therapy."

CHAPTER 2

Reincarnation and Christianity

It's amazing to me that Christianity appears to be against the concept of reincarnation. However, according to a Harris Poll conducted in 2011, 24% of Americans believe in reincarnation and 79% believe their soul survives death, and 76% of Americans according to the American Religious Identification Survey (ARIS) claim to be Christians.

Let's go back to the early Christian movement, where reincarnation and preexistence was a concept that was pretty well taken for granted. Jesus himself talked about John the Baptist as the return of Elias (Matt. 11:14; Mark 9:11–13).

Jesus told us that even the least among us could do what he had done—and even greater things. Jesus said this because he knew, through his own past lives and having returned many times, that the "God spirit" is in all of us. This makes anything possible, if we can truly understand what Jesus was trying to convey. Further proof is the fact that almost all of the principal founders of what would eventually become Christianity were part of the Essenes, who taught preexistence and reincarnation.

Remember that Jesus was an Essene rabbi. Essenes believed in preexistence and reincarnation. There is no denying it; it's historical fact. Jesus believed and taught reincarnation and karma.

For centuries the Jewish people believed that their spiritual leaders were reborn. Evidence of this can be found in the Dead Sea scrolls, early Christian and Jewish writings, the New Testament, and the writings of ancient historians.

The origin of resurrection and reincarnation in Jewish and Christian belief systems began with the Babylonian exile, a period when the Jews in Israel were conquered and taken captive to Babylon. Later, in 539 BC, Babylon itself was conquered by the Persians, who installed a Zoroastrian theocracy throughout the defeated Babylonian Empire. It was then that the Zoroastrian religion and its belief in resurrection began to take hold in Judaism.

Christianity, in turn, inherited the concept of resurrection from Judaism. In fact, it was the Zoroastrian religion that was the source of belief in resurrection, angels, the afterlife, rewards and punishments, the soul's immortality, and the last judgment. This is where Christianity's core belief system came from.

The first-century Jewish historian, Flavius Josephus, wrote that the Pharisees—the Jewish sect that founded rabbinic Judaism, to which Paul once belonged—believed in reincarnation. Josephus records that the Essenes of the Dead Sea scrolls believed that the soul is both immortal and preexistent before birth.

The book of Enoch, which is considered the oldest text of Jewish mysticism, was also found with the scrolls. Since evidence shows that Jewish mysticism existed in the third century BC, as Enoch indicates, then it would certainly have existed in first-century Israel. The ideas of divine union and reincarnation can both be found in early Christianity. It's quite obvious that reincarnation went to the very heart of Jesus's message.

The first great leader of the early orthodox church was Origen (AD 185–254), who was the first person since Paul to develop a system of theology around Jesus's teachings. Origen was a strong defender of preexistence and reincarnation.

Preexistence is the religious concept that the soul is not created at birth. Rather, before birth the soul existed in heaven or in a past life on earth—which we know to be fact from the thousands of people who have pre-birth memories today.

Origen taught that preexistence is found in Hebrew Scriptures and in the teaching of Jesus.

Origen was a disciple of Clement of Alexandria, who was a disciple of thepostle Peter. Clement and Origen wrote about receiving the teachings of Jesus as handed down from thepostles. One of these teachings was the concept of physical and spiritual rebirth. The existence of these secret teachings and mysteries from Jesus is recorded in the Bible. Here are some of those instances.

"He replied, 'The knowledge of the secrets of the kingdom of heaven has been given to you, but not to them. Whoever has will be given more and he will have abundance" (Matt. 13:11–12).

"I have become its servant by the commission God gave me to present to you the word of God in its fullness—the mystery that has been kept hidden for ages and generations, but is now disclosed to the saints. To them God has chosen to make among the Gentiles the glorious riches of this mystery, which is Christ in you, the hope of glory" (Col. 1:25–27).

"Listen, I tell you a mystery. We will not sleep, but we will all be changed" (1 Cor. 15:51).

The concept of preexistence and reincarnation were the secret teachings of Jesus, until they were outlawed by the Roman church in AD 553. It was during this time that the Roman church aggressively destroyed competing teachings and so-called heresies within the church. Along with the destruction of these teachings on preexistence and reincarnation came the murder of anyone who stood in the way of the Roman church's control. After this murderous rampage by the church, reincarnation became an enemy concept to Western Judeo-Christianity.

Gregory, the Bishop of Nyssa, gave us the five reasons that reincarnation was declared heresy:

1. It seems to minimize Christian salvation.

2. It is in conflict with the resurrection of the body.

3. It creates an unnatural separation between body and soul.

4. It is built on speculative use of Christian Scriptures.

5. There is no recollection of previous lives.

But in 1945, writings containing many of the secrets of early Christianity were unearthed in northern Egypt. This was an area where many Christians fled when the Romans invaded Israel. The writings revealed more information about the concept of reincarnation from the sect of Christians called Gnostics. As stated above, this sect was ultimately destroyed by the Roman orthodox church; their followers were burned at the stake, and their writings were wiped out. Those writings included some long lost gospels of Matthew, Mark, Luke, and John.

The early Christians were spiritual critics of the orthodox church because of what they saw as a vulgarization of Christianity. The orthodox church stressed blind faith and obedience-or-death, while the Gnostic Christian church stressed spiritual knowledge and understanding. The secret teachings of Jesus emphasized spiritual resurrection rather than physical resurrection. A lot of these texts are at odds with the Bible today. Most Christians are not even aware of these original Christian beliefs. If anyone was to truly think about it, he would conclude that these ancient texts—rather than the rewritten Bible of today—hold the true meaning and intent of Jesus.

The early Gnostic Christians believed, as Jesus did, that reincarnation is the true interpretation of the resurrection, meaning that resurrection is of the spirit, not the body. The early Christians claimed that they possessed the correct definition of the resurrection, based on Jesus's secret teachings handed down by the apostles. The existence of a secret tradition can be found in the New Testament.

The finding of these writings in 1945 was truly an amazing discovery. Undisturbed since their concealment almost two thousand years ago, these writings ranked in importance equal to the Dead Sea scrolls, which were discovered two years later. These so-called secret teachings concerning life and death are strikingly similar to what we know about near-death experiences.

Reincarnation and the Secret Teachings of Jesus

There are many Bible verses that affirm the reality of reincarnation. Let's look at some of them here.

The episode in the Bible where Jesus identified John the Baptist as the reincarnation of Elijah the prophet is one of the clearest statements that Jesus made concerning reincarnation. "For all the prophets and the law have prophesied until John. And if you are willing to receive it, he is Elijah who has come (Matt. 11:13–14).

In this passage, Jesus clearly identified John the Baptist as the reincarnation of Elijah the prophet. Later in Matthew's gospel, Jesus stated it again, and the disciples asked, "Why then do the scribes say that Elijah must come first." Before the Messiah. Jesus answered them and said, 'Elijah indeed is to come and will restore things. But I say to you, Elijah has come already and they did not know him, but did to him whatever they wished. So also shall the Son of Man suffer at their hand." Then the disciples understood that he had spoken of John the Baptist. (Matt. 17:10–13).

In very explicit language, Jesus identified John the Baptist as the reincarnation of Elijah. Even the disciples of Jesus understood what Jesus was saying. This identification of John as the reincarnation of Elijah is very important when it comes to Bible prophecy. By identifying John with Elijah, Jesus identified himself as the Messiah. The Hebrew Scriptures mentioned specific signs that would precede the coming of the Messiah. One of them was that Elijah would return first.

"Behold I will send you Elijah the prophet, before the coming of the great and dreadful day of the Lord" (Mal. 4:5). This is one of the Messianic promises from God that is found in the Bible. These "John is Elijah" references clearly show the reality of reincarnation. There are two important conclusions we can draw from this:

1. The Hebrew Scriptures prophesied that Elijah himself—not someone like him or someone in the same ministry as his—would return before the advent of the Messiah.

2. Jesus declared John to be Elijah when he stated that Elijah had come.

Based on these conclusions alone, one of the two statements below must be true:

1. John was himself Elijah, which means that Elijah reincarnated as John the Baptist. If this is true, then reincarnation must belong once again in the Christian teachings. It also means that the concept of dead bodies coming out of their graves on judgment day can be discarded, or

2. John was *not* Elijah reincarnate, which means that Elijah himself did not return. If this is true, then one of the two statements below is true:

   a. Malachi's prophecy concerning Elijah's return to life before the coming of the Messiah failed to happen. This means that God does not keep his promises and that the Bible is fallible, or

   b. Jesus was not the Messiah.

Based on the logic so far, only one of the following conclusions is true:

1. Reincarnation is a reality, or

2. Jesus was not the Messiah, or

3. Bible prophecies are not reliable.

There is no way around this reasoning. Only one of the above options can be true, and because Jesus made a direct statement that John is Elijah, the only option left is that John was the reincarnation of Elijah.

The following is another verse supporting preexistence: "'I tell you the truth,' Jesus answered, 'before Abraham was born, I am'" (John 8:58). In this verse, Jesus told his followers that he existed before Abraham was even born. This would only be true if Jesus existed before he was born. Jesus had a human nature along with a divine nature. Therefore, it does not take a lot of faith to believe that all humans preexisted.

Reincarnation and Divine Justice

The law of divine justice is practically a universal religious concept. In eastern religions, this law is called *karma*. This law of divine justice is equal to the concept of reincarnation. This law of living by the sword and dying by the sword is the principal of reincarnation. In other words, this law of divine justice is the law of reincarnation.

Only reincarnation can resolve the justice taught by phrases like "reaping what we sow," "an eye for an eye," and "live by the sword and die by the sword." This universal law of God explains why some people are born under favorable conditions and others are born under unfavorable conditions. It is the mechanics of birth and rebirth. Reincarnation is the missing link to understanding the secret and mystical teachings of Jesus.

This law of God is the key to the following parable of Jesus: "Again, it (the kingdom of heaven) will be like a man going on a journey, which called his servants and entrusted his property to them. To one he gave five talents of money, to another two talents, and to another one talent, each according to his ability" (Matt. 25:14–15).

The idea that God gives people varying resources at birth—each according to his ability—is the heart of reincarnation and the law of divine justice. The great father Origen used this very parable to teach preexistence and reincarnation. "The soul has neither beginning nor end ... [They] come into this world strengthened by victories or weakened by the defeats of their previous lives" (Origen, *De Principiis*).

It's important to understand that the idea of bodily resurrection was not an orthodox Jewish concept. It was a doctrine that Hellenized (Greek-influenced) Jews held. Paul was a Hellenized Pharisee who converted to Christianity and rejected Judaism, of which Jesus was a follower. The Pharisees and Jesus both believed and taught reincarnation.

So Paul renounced his Judaism, the Law, and reincarnation. Paul started teaching the Gentiles the alien concept of bodily resurrection, dead corpses coming out of the ground. I think the only reason Paul starting teaching this concept was that he misunderstood Christ's teachings of the resurrection.

Paul himself was in conflict with the church. Pauline Christianity became Christianity minus the Judaism of Jesus. When we add to that his adoption of Greek culture, we see that Paul provided the world with a major historical misunderstanding of Christianity. The Christianity established in Rome replaced the Jerusalem Christianity established by Jesus and the Twelve.

The foreign influences that Paul introduced into the teachings of Jesus are so massive that scholars say that Paul hijacked Christianity from the apostles of Jesus. However, my belief is that Paul never intended his letters to become God's Word, the Word on which the Christian religion would be based. But with Jesus crucified, his followers were searching for anybody who would carry on where Jesus had left off, and Paul stepped up to the plate.

You may wonder why Paul chose not to invest his time in learning from those who knew Jesus, lived with Jesus, and taught with Jesus. Instead, Paul believed his vision of Jesus was superior to those who truly knew him. So Paul proclaimed himself an apostle, created his own version of Christianity, and chose to be in conflict with the church that had been established based on Jesus's teachings.

There is *compelling historical evidence* that Jesus taught his closest disciples about reincarnation. Also, the historical fact that Origen had Christian Gnostic ties and was a believer in preexistence and reincarnation shows without a doubt that reincarnation was part of the early church's teachings in Jerusalem. Origen was the most influential Christian theologian after Paul. Historical evidence shows that the early Jerusalem church did not view bodily resurrection as part of the scheme of redemption. Again, bodily resurrection was a foreign concept to traditional Judaism and Christian Judaism.

Reincarnation was a concept taught by Jesus and the early church in Jerusalem. Reincarnation is a concept of orthodox Judaism to this day. Reincarnation should be the doctrine of every Christian. Perhaps there is a divine reason for the recent discoveries of the Dead Sea scrolls and the writings of early Jerusalem Christians discovered in Upper Egypt. Both proclaim reincarnation, not bodily resurrection, to be the true faith.

Reincarnation in Many Sacred Texts

Here are more references to reincarnation.

> "You keep count of my wanderings: put my tears into your flask, into your record" (Psalm 56:8–9 NJPS (*Tanak: The Holy Scriptures*).

> "Then I said, 'Behold, I come; in the volume of the book it is written of me: I delight to do your will, O my God; yes. Your law is within my heart" (Ps. 40:7–8 AB).

> "You had scrutinized my every action, all were recorded in your book, my days listed and determined, even before the first of them occurred" (Ps. 139:16 JB).

> "The book in which man's actions, good and bad, are recorded, the book of Life" Rev. 20:12, NJB).

> "And Jesus opened up to (the disciples) the meaning of the hidden way, the Holy Breath, of the light that cannot fail. He told them all about the Book of Life, the Rolls of Graphgael, and the Book of God's Remembrance, where all thoughts and words of men are written down" (*The Aquarian Gospel of Jesus the Christ*, 158:3–4)

It's obvious that there are many references to the recording and remembering of our lifetime of words and actions.

I know I seem to be repeating myself, but it's very important for all of us to understand how reincarnation and other teachings of Jesus were removed from Christian doctrines. We must look to the development of the Roman Catholic Church.

Many people think that the Bible as we know it was created by Jesus and the apostles during the first century AD, but this is definitely not true. For a long period of time—for hundreds of years—the early Christians had no such concept as a closed canon of Scripture (a collection of books viewed as final). Actually, it was quite the opposite. During the creative years of Christianity, people felt free to compose new Scriptures—psalms, odes, proverbs, and letters—that they felt inspired them. During these early years, Christianity was much more of a supernatural religion, and there was a great deal of emphasis placed on experiencing the spiritual realm or "kingdom of God."

We have a great number of spiritual leaders today who write and teach, yet their work is not recognized as Scripture. I say, "Why not?" God can inspire anyone at any time to write great things. This great, intelligent force that flows through everything would never have limited men spiritually. Nor would God allow only certain books that were authorized by the church for us to follow. This type of organized religion is what Jesus was against. His objection to the organized church at that time led to his eventually being crucified.

Now, let's move forward to the first three hundred years after Jesus's death, when many factions of Christianity flourished. Some believed in reincarnation, and some did not. The different beliefs were in constant conflict. There were two major movements in early Christianity: the Paulinians and the Gnostics.

In AD 325 Emperor Constantine laid down the foundation for the present form of the church. He obviously did this more to have power over the people than because he was a true believer. Some of the records from that council are incomplete, but it *is* known that the Gnostic Christians were not allowed to participate in the meeting.

Their petitions were burned without opening them, and reincarnation was removed from the Bible, even though it was part of Jesus's original teachings. This was an early attempt to unify Christianity with one set of beliefs for all Christians to follow.

Therefore, the Council of Nicaea formulated and established a new doctrine from which reincarnation had been removed.

Again in AD 553 reincarnation was dropped from Christian doctrine at the Fifth Ecumenical Council at Constantinople. At that time, the Roman Empire was divided into two parts: the Eastern Empire at Constantinople and the Western Empire at Rome. It has been noted historically that the rejection of reincarnation, with its possibility of past and future lives, was personally motivated by Justinian, the emperor of the Eastern Empire, and his wife, Theodora.

Although the vote on reincarnation at the Council relied on bishops from both the Eastern and Western Empires, only two bishops from Rome came to Constantinople to vote. Two previous popes had been murdered after they had denounced the dropping of the belief in reincarnation from the Bible and Jesus's teachings. Many of the Roman bishops were afraid to vote against the wishes of Justinian. After the vote, all Bibles throughout both empires were confiscated, burned, and rewritten.

Just think about how these power-hungry people, in their attempt for control, edited and changed the original teachings of Jesus and the Bible. I believe that, at the time, the church wanted Christians to think that they had only one lifetime in which to do good deeds, so they would likely be frightened into following the rules set by the church. As Christians, we should be appalled by these actions, but it seems that, even with all the evidence, Christians have a totally blind faith in following texts that are known to have been manipulated. Again, churches are hindering you and the spirit that's within you. Man started making up all these rules and restrictions about how to make the journey to God. Different religions came into being, attempting to deny and restrict the mystical, spiritual nature of man.

Another idea pushed by the church is this: if you don't believe in Jesus, you will go to hell, and you won't have eternal life. Are they telling me that the intelligent force that flows through all of us is going to let little babies, in countries that haven't heard of Jesus, die and go to hell? *I think not.* That concept borders on insanity, and those who teach it should be ashamed of themselves.

Another area I have become curious about is this. After studying the four Gospels of the New Testament, I was surprised that each of them only devoted a short chapter to the teachings and activities of Jesus after the resurrection. Let's be real here. Wouldn't you think that, if someone rose from the dead, the event would immediately become the most dramatic event ever for humanity? Don't you think everyone would have been obsessed with recording every word, every movement, and every deed of the person raised? The fact that someone had risen from the dead should have become the only focus of writers at that time. There should have been books written about this unbelievable time in human history. But the New Testament simply says that there were many other things that Jesus did as he continued to appear to the disciples.

Another Bible story falls to the wayside. The *Gospel of Judas Iscariot* has been authenticated, and it proves that Judas did exactly what Jesus asked him to do: call the authorities and let them know where Jesus was hiding. Jesus wanted to be executed so that his spirit could be released from his body. Jesus knew he would come back again, if he chose, through reincarnation.

Needless to say, even with all the deletions and changes to the original text, the Bible still has a tremendous amount of spiritual wisdom that all of us can benefit from. But remember that the Bible has been written and rewritten many times by different people with different agendas, both political and personal. God, the intelligent force that flows through everything, never intended for man to make up various religions and then pronounce death to anyone who did not believe in their version of the truth. Jesus said it best when he said that there is no need for a church or organized religion, because God lives in all of us.

Even after all the death and destruction that the church had caused, belief in reincarnation still didn't disappear. Early in the thirteenth century, the pope launched a crusade against the Cathers—a Christian sect in Italy and southern France that had followed the original teachings of Jesus, which included reincarnation—which murdered every last one of them. The Spanish Inquisition followed, with death to anyone who deviated from strict church doctrine.

The truth is, people who believed in reincarnation took greater personal responsibility for their own spiritual development. This undermined the authority and power of the developing church, which was, at the time, a money-making machine that placed great pressure upon the population to attend church and to contribute offerings in the form of tithes. Believers in reincarnation relied less on the influence and control of priests, confessionals, and rituals to ward off eternal damnation, and this struck fear into the churches. None of these church trappings were part of Jesus's original teaching. They were added by men who developed the religion to gain power over the people.

Look at the protestant Bible. The protestants removed books from the Bible about two hundred years ago. These books were called the Apocrypha. Today most Protestants think these disputed books are of the Catholic church, but the truth of the matter is that the books of the Apocrypha have for centuries been included in the Greek Orthodox, Syrian, Russian, Armenian, Egyptian, and other ancient churches and their Bibles. Translations of most of these books can be found in the Dead Sea scrolls. The original Greek translation of the Old Testament was made in Alexandria around 200 BC. These books have now vanished from protestant Bibles in the United States.

Reincarnation has never been in conflict with the teachings of Jesus. It has only been in conflict with the control wielded by the church.

The biblical defense of reincarnation leads us to the following conclusions:

1. The religious concept of a massive, worldwide reanimation of decayed corpses at the end of time is a foreign concept that originated in ancient Persia.

2. The massive, worldwide reanimation of corpses is bizarre, unnatural, and repulsive.

3. Reincarnation was widely believed by the people of Israel in the days of Jesus and by people all around the world.

4. All Hebrew and Christian scriptures support reincarnation: the Bible, the Dead Sea scrolls, the Christian Gnostic gospels, the Torah, the Hebrew Bible, the Apocrypha, the Kabbalah, and the Zohar.

5. Many of the biblical references to resurrection refer to spiritual regeneration while already physically alive, rather than reanimation of corpses on the so-called last day.

6. Reincarnation is the rebirth of a person's spirit into a new body that is born again as an infant. Resurrection is the spiritual awakening of a living person's spirit of the Holy Spirit.

7. The Bible records Jesus himself as teaching reincarnation to his followers.

8. Early Christians in Jerusalem believed in and taught reincarnation, until it was declared a heresy by the Church of Rome.

9. Reincarnation has been a tenet in orthodox Judaism for thousands of years, and continues today.

10. The concept of reincarnation is supported by many near-death experiences and by thousands of past-life regressions.

11. Again I say that reincarnation should be a doctrine accepted by every follower of Jesus Christ.

Jesus was an incarnate human who achieved enlightenment. Jesus was totally aware of his past lives, and he mentions this in his teachings.

Jesus knew who he truly was and how he fit into the grand design for humanity. Jesus was persecuted for his beliefs by those who feared his power. I believe that Jesus's truest gift to mankind was that he simply remembered his past lives and let us know that God lives inside all of us. Jesus tried to pass this knowledge on through his ministry, but as you can see, the message has been distorted and changed. That knowledge threatened men in power, and especially the religious zealots.

CHAPTER 3

Jesus and Buddha

Was Jesus Buddha reincarnated?

I know this sounds like I have lost touch with reality, but hear me out. I think you will find this information mind-altering to your belief system.

I am sure most of you know who Edgar Cayce was. If you don't, please look him up. Some people called him the sleeping prophet. During one of his trances, he received the following revelations concerning the connection between Buddha and Jesus.

Christian Gnosticism is the highest form of Christianity, according to Cayce's revelations and most Bible scholars. A close study of Christian Gnosticism shows that this early form of Christianity was almost identical to Buddhism. Remember that Buddhism has been around since six hundred years before Christ.

For example, both religions teach reincarnation, the oneness of all things, the divine light, the existence of an afterlife in various forms, the Gnostic goal for every human being to achieve Christhood (identical to the goal of attaining Buddhahood), the distinction between Jesus the human being and Christ the spirit of human-divine unity (like the distinction between Buddha the human being and the Dharmakaya, the clear light of ultimate reality), belief in the ancient concept of Karma, and the importance of doing good deeds. This is only a partial list.

Now let's look at the life experiences of Jesus and Siddhartha Gautama, also known as the Buddha.

The basic teachings and the lives of the Buddha and the Christ are so similar that it is hard to believe they are not the same person. Buddhism teaches that practicing good religious and moral behavior can lead to kingdom of God or enlightenment. To obtain enlightenment, a person will be subjected to the cycle of reincarnation. As it was with Jesus, the Buddha had a community of disciples to carry on his teachings.

The Buddha was born of the virgin Mahamaya, who was considered the Queen of Heaven. Jesus was born of the Virgin Mary. Mary and Mahamaya both gave birth to their sons among strangers. Both were visited by wise men who recognized the divinity of the children.

Both Jesus and Buddha were presented in the temple as infants for baptism. The hymns sung at both annunciations resembled each other.

In childhood, both had a problem with their teachers.

Jesus and Buddha were considered to be divine beings. Both taught people how to free themselves from the cycle of birth, death, and rebirth.

The missions of both Buddha and Jesus were proclaimed by voices from heaven.

Both fasted in the wilderness and were tempted. Supernatural beings ministered to each of them.

Both called their disciples with the command, "Follow me." Both sent out disciples to spread the news of their teachings. Both performed miracles, healed the sick, fed five hundred men from a small basket of bread, and walked on water.

Buddha was about thirty years old when he began his ministry, about the same age as Jesus. He had a band of disciples who accompanied him and traveled from place to place and preached to large groups, as Jesus did.

Buddha formulated certain commandments hundreds of years before Christ: not to steal, not to kill, not to commit adultery. Similar teachings are attributed to Jesus: do not commit adultery, do not murder, do not steal, do not give false testimony, honor your father and mother (Luke 18:20). Christ ignored the literal interpretation of Moses and emphasized a spiritualized interpretation of the Law taken as a whole—to practice unconditional love. This is what Buddha did with the current teachings of his days.

Buddha preached on the Holy Hill. Jesus preached his sermon on "the Mount." The phraseology of the sermons of Buddha and the sermon of Jesus is the same in many areas. Both Buddha and Jesus compared themselves to husbandmen sowing seeds. The parable of the prodigal son is found in both Buddhist and Christian scriptures. So is the account of the man who was born blind. Both used the mustard seed as a simile for smallness. Buddha taught: perishable is the city built of sand. Jesus taught: a foolish man builds his house upon the sand. Both speak of the rain that falls on the just and on the unjust.

A reformed prostitute, Mary Magdalene, followed Jesus. A reformed prostitute, Ambapali, followed Buddha.

It is written that Buddha crushed a serpent's head. Crushing the head of the serpent was also a Messianic prophecy described in Genesis in the garden of Eden.

Buddha preached the establishment of a kingdom of righteousness, as did Jesus. Buddha taught chastity, temperance, tolerance, compassion, love, and the equality of all, as Jesus did.

The story of Nicodemus, the ruler who came to Jesus by night, is the same story as the rich man who came to Buddha at night.

Both men proclaimed kingdoms not of this world. The eternal life promised by Jesus corresponds to the eternal peace promised by Buddha.

Both were transfigured on a mount.

Both made triumphal entries: Christ into Jerusalem and Buddha into Rajagriba.

Buddha was considered the good shepherd, the carpenter, the infinite and everlasting. Buddha was called the savior of the world, supreme being, and the eternal one, just as Jesus was.

There is a legend of a traitor connected to both of them.

Buddha is to return to earth to restore the world to order and happiness, and so is Jesus.

Both are judges of the dead.

Buddha commanded his disciples to preach his gospel to all men. Christ commanded his disciples to do the same.

In 1947 early Christian documents were discovered. One of the documents was the gospel of Thomas, which is considered by scholars to be the earliest gospel ever written and the most reliable. The gospel of Thomas talks about a type of Christianity that is identical to the teachings of Buddhism. It describes Jesus teaching the disciples how to become free from reincarnation.

Let's look at a few more:

1. Do to others as you have them do to you (Luke 6:31). Consider others as yourself (Dhammapada 10:1).

2. If someone slaps you on one cheek, turn to them the other also (Luke 6:29). If anyone should give you a blow with his hand, you should abandon any desires and utter no evil words (Majjhima Nikaya 21:6).

3. But to you are listening I say: Love your enemies, do good to those who hate you, bless those who curse you, pray for those who mistreat you (Luke 6:27–28). Hatreds do not ever cease in this world by hating, but by love: this is the eternal truth. Overcome anger by love, overcome evil by good, overcome the liar by truth (Dhammapada 1.5; 17.3).

4. He will reply, truly I tell you, whatever you did not do for one of the least of these, you did not do for me (Matthew 25:45). If you do not tend one another, then who is there to tend to you? (Vinaya, Mahavagga 8:26:3).

5. Why do you look at the speck of sawdust in your brother's eye and pay no attention to the plank in your own eye? How can you say to your brother, Brother, let me take the speck out of your eye, when you yourself fail to see the plank in your own eye? You hypocrite, first take the plank out of your eye, and then you will see clearly to remove the speck from your brother's eye (Luke 6:41–42). The faults of others are easier to see than one's own, for they are sifted like chaff, but one's own faults are hard to see. This is the cheat who hides his dice and shows the dice of his opponent, calling attention to the other's shortcomings, continually thinking of accusing him (Udanavarga 27:1).

6. Your father in heaven makes his sun rise on the evil and on the good and sends rain on the righteous and on the unrighteous (Matthew 5:45). That great cloud rains on all whether their nature is superior or inferior. The light of the sun illuminates the whole world, both him who does well and him who does ill (Saddharma Pundarika Sutra 5).

7. Everyone who believes in me will never die (John 11:26). Those who have faith in me, love for me, are all headed for heaven or beyond (Majjhirma Nilaya 72:15).

8. When the devil had finished every test, he departed from him until an opportune time (Luke 4:13). The demon followed behind him, seeking an opportunity to harm him. But he found no opportunity whatsoever and went away discouraged (Lalitavistara Sutra 18).

9. Although the doors were shut, Jesus came and stood among them (John 20:26). He goes unhindered through a wall (Anguttara Nikaya 3:60).

I can go on forever, but it would take another book. The teachings of Buddha and Christ are identical in every aspect.

How could this possibly happen?

In my opinion, there are only two ways this could have happened.

One theory is that Jesus was the reincarnation of Buddha, and everything that Jesus said and did had already been said and done by Buddha. Every healing or miracle, even the ability to walk on water, everything that Christians thought were acts by Jesus Christ, were all acts of the Buddha—six hundred years earlier.

The other possibility is this: if Jesus was not the reincarnate Buddha, then Jesus must have studied Buddhism, read every word the Buddha had proclaimed, and claimed it to be his own. Thus Christianity is following the format and belief systems created by Buddha. Christians today may be following the Buddha's teachings, not those of Jesus Christ.

I believe, as some scholars believe, in the first theory. First came Kistna with his teachings and miracles, and then came Buddha with his teachings and miracles (which sound almost identical to Kistna's), and last came Jesus, whose teachings and miracles could have been taken out of Buddha's handbook. In my opinion, Jesus Christ was the reincarnation of Kistna and Buddha, because the original teachings that these great spiritual leaders provided have not changed. There is a continuance of thought that has flowed through each of them, furthering the cause of enlightenment for thousands of years of human history.

CHAPTER 4

The Purpose and End of Reincarnation

The purpose of reincarnation is to understand that we are evolving spirits. Through reincarnation we keep returning until we have learned enough life lessons and gained enough experience from earth life that reincarnation is no longer necessary—like graduation. Reincarnation is not a goal. Eternal life means never having to die anymore. This was the message that Jesus was trying to convey: that we should follow his direction to be the best we can be, and once we reach a certain understanding, we will have eternal life—meaning that we will not have to return to earth in human form. That is the goal: to overcome death and rebirth. Reincarnation is the method and means to attain this goal.

When you understand your true nature, you can free yourself from limitations and accept full responsibility for your actions. The need to experience and learn those lessons through physical existence on earth will no longer be necessary.

As we have allowed our lives to become more complicated, we have started to value material possessions. Things like the most expensive car, the best vacation, the biggest house, or the best school have come to define who we are and the level of our self-worth. Society progressively makes up more and more rules to try to control every aspect of an individual's life. This is the case, today more than ever, with the expansion of big government and socialism as a means of control. Some people may have thought it would be easier to allow others to be responsible for directing us all, telling us what to do and what to think, while excessively taxing the working people of our society and giving the money to causes of the government's choice, not our own, and basically deciding how we should live our lives.

At some point, we, the people, began to give up on taking personal responsibility for ourselves and for our actions. We used this control by government and others as an excuse for our misfortunes. It gave us someone else to blame.

We must finally learn that everything that has happened to us—good or bad, past or present—has happened because we allowed it to happen in some way. I am not saying that we knew directly that we were creating a bad situation, but somehow, along the way, we have allowed things to happen that have created an undesirable situation. Once we embrace this realization, life takes on a whole different meaning. We have no more excuses. We are in control of ourselves!

The End of Reincarnation

Some people feel that they must be on their final incarnation, simply because they are spiritual and have little interest in the material world. I have done a lot of research in this area, and that is not how reincarnation works.

The goal of evolution is not to escape from the physical world, despite what many others teach. The end of reincarnation is not some sort of reward for good behavior. Human existence is not a prison or place of torment from which only the worthy can gain freedom and liberation.

We incarnate because we want to and choose to. We keep doing it precisely because we want to come to terms with it. We know that in each lifetime we will probably spend several decades not remembering who we are, not remembering our eternal home, buying into the illusion of separation, and experiencing fear. This is the very stuff that inspires us to become more conscious.

Completion occurs when it matters not whether you are incarnate or discarnate: you see through the veil of illusion and you always feel at home.

CHAPTER 5

Soul Relationships

Are You an Old Soul?

Have you ever been told that you are an "old soul"? Most of us don't have a clue what this means, but it sounds good and mysterious and makes us feel like we are superior to others.

Being an old soul implies that the soul has been around longer than the body and that we may have some special knowledge or wisdom that sets us apart from everyone else.

Chronologically speaking, we are all old souls. Regression evidence shows that all souls were created at the same time. Some souls have lived more lifetimes than others. These souls can be said to have more experience than others.

Some souls understand and pass a subject the first time, while others must repeat a subject to understand.

The fact that we are still here tells us that we have further lessons to learn. So, being an old soul isn't a status symbol; it's just a fact of life.

The progression of the soul through reincarnation goes in stages:

1. The first stage, as an *infant* soul, involves learning about the physical existence, life and death, and the need for nurturing.

2. The second stage is a *baby* soul. It's learning about society, culture, and community. It needs structure, belonging, and the opportunity to play a role.

3. The third stage is a *young* soul. It has learned about free will and self-determination, taking charge of its own destiny.

4. The fourth stage is a *mature* soul. It's learning about coexistence and interrelatedness, taking responsibility for its relationships, honoring difference and otherness.

5. The fifth and final stage is the *old* soul. This soul is searching for balance and completion and has an urge to "pass the torch" before the end of reincarnation.

The Old Soul Routine

There are many old souls around us. Most of us know of them. Old souls seem to be self-assured. They are generally relaxed and comfortable in their own skin. That's not to say that they have no issues; many clearly do.

Old souls emanate a calm, steady quality that has substance, depth, or gravitas. In comparison, young souls can appear frantic and superficial.

This inner calm and depth is also evident in the old soul's eyes. Whereas young souls cannot make eye contact for long, old souls are unafraid to look others in the eyes and see their hearts.

Compared to other souls, old souls are generally relaxed and philosophical about life, at ease with themselves and others. They don't really care about material attachments. They tend to be drawn to a quiet life away from the noise of the city. The old soul is more a citizen of the world than a person wedded to one place.

But don't be drawn into the old-soul routine, as it can cause problems. Attempting to judge another human being's spiritual level has many pitfalls. Who are we to judge someone else's career, appearance, social status, outward signs of spirituality, or intuitive feelings? That would be assuming a role to which we have no right. Nor do we have the wisdom to do so. We are not God!

We often find it easier to criticize faults and weaknesses in others than to find talents, strengths, and positive character traits in others.

We must always try to look for the good in others. What we seek, we will find. If we are looking for faults in others, then all we will find is faults. If we are looking for the good in others, then all we will find is good. This saying is true in all circumstances.

Some Famous Old Souls

Old souls who become famous tend to do so by virtue of their mastery, insight, and wisdom rather than ambition.

Many of the finest minds in history have been old souls: Marcus Aurelius (121–180), Leonardo da Vinci (1452–1519), and Carl Jung (1875–1961).

In the arts, we have the composer J. S. Bach (1685–1750), the painter Paul Gauguin (1848–1903) (now apparently reincarnated as artist Peter Tee Kamp), and the writers Walt Whitman (1819–1892) and William Blake (1757–1827).

In the acting profession, there are numerous old souls who are brilliant at playing characters that are essentially younger souls—mainly because there aren't that many scripts featuring old-soul characters. Consider, for example, Anthony Hopkins playing Hannibal Lecter or Ben Kingsley in Sexy Beast. Morgan Freeman is well-known for the gravitas he brings to every role. Clint Eastwood's acting reveals a mix of warrior-soul combativeness with old-soul detachment, but it is as a director that he has achieved mastery.

Finally, many of the world's great spiritual teachers have been late-stage old souls passing on their wisdom: Gurdjieff (1866–1949), Jiddu Krishnamurti (1895–1986), Ramana Maharishi (1879–1950), Anandamayi Ma (1896–1962), the Dalai Lama, Billy Graham, Wayne Dyer, Deepak Chopra, and many others who continue to show us the way.

Soul Mates

The idea of soul mates may sound romantic, but there is no evidence to support the idea that, in the entire universe, there is but one soul who is your true mate. Through thousands of years of our existence, there have been many souls that we have loved. We have been bound by great friendships and have had a variety of experiences through many lifetimes together.

When meeting a soul-friend for the first time in this current lifetime, we may feel an immediate friendship that stirs up deep emotions. We may feel little need to maintain a protective facade or to play the social games that have become part of our daily lives with each other.

Soul mates are the special people in our lives. These are people we have loved, helped, and shared previous lives with, striving toward understanding and bonding with them.

A soul mate is someone we feel profoundly connected to, and our communication with them is effortless. This kind of relationship is so important to the soul that many have said there is nothing more precious in life.

I feel that there are four distinctly different kinds of soul mates. Each kind has its own unique characteristics that make the person unmistakably distinguishable from others who have come into our lives.

Teacher Soul Mates

These people usually form the most difficult soul relationships with us. They are here to help us learn very uncomfortable lessons. These souls have agreed to be the "bad guy," the rough teacher. We sometimes have trouble understanding the connection or love with these soul mates, because they challenge us constantly, and we have difficultly achieving any common ground with them. They force us into growth situations where we are obliged to change. They rarely stay in our lives for long, but we remember them forever.

Companion Soul Mates

Usually these souls are here to help us along our path. Their help can be in the form of a chance encounter, a comment made, a kind word, or other various means—and always when we need it most. We meet companion soul mates every day in different situations. We may see them as strangers or acquaintances who offer good advice or who listen when we need to talk. These soul mates are the encouragers who help us try something new or different in our lives. They make us feel better about ourselves.

We may spend only a brief time with these people without a serious bond. Perhaps in previous lifetimes we helped these souls, and now they are returning the favor.

Twin Soul Mates

These people are the ones with whom we have shared a special and loving relationship over many lifetimes. We feel a complete, natural, and open energy with them. When we first meet this soul mate, it's like meeting an old friend. There is a connection, a comfortable feeling that almost seems like starting a relationship right where it left off in a previous lifetime.

Twin soul mates are usually close family members, special friends, and people who understand us without judging us. There is often a spiritual, psychic connection with this soul mate. Much of the time, we don't even need words to communicate, for our souls are in tune at a telepathic level, and we intuitively know their feelings. We often marry this soul mate.

Twin Flame Soul Mates

The twin flame soul mate takes it a step further than twin soul mates. There is a deep and meaningful spiritual bond that creates a special rapport between twin flame soul mates. There is an energy that flows between them. They know on some level that they have known the other person forever. They belong together and cannot be separated.

This special connection between twin flame soul mates is something they will not experience with anyone else. It's a shame, but we do not meet our twin soul mate in every lifetime. I think it's because we need time to assist others—to be healers, teachers, guides, and spiritual adviser—without the distraction of our twin flame soul mate.

I feel that the important issue is to make each relationship the best it can be. We must honor, nurture, and allow our relations with others to grow. This will be empowering for the growth of both souls.

Reincarnating with Soul Friends

Research has shown that we seem to reincarnate in groups. Our paths with others from past lifetimes seem to cross again and again. In some instances, it is possible that two people have made a commitment to work together over several lifetimes. Having a soul friend can be one of the most rewarding experiences possible.

Specialness of the Soul Relationship

Several aspects of the soul relationship make it special: the respect we show each other, not taking comments to heart, courtesy and patience, and listening and allowing each other to have differing opinions. There is openness in talking about our feelings. We are able to allow each other the right to argue or even to get angry, knowing that it doesn't change the love we have for each other. If we become the person we want our friends to be, our lives will be right in all the areas that really count.

CHAPTER 6

Karma

Karma is a Sanskrit word that literally means "action."

Karma describes the connection between actions and the resulting forces as follows: good positive actions, lead to good positive results, while negative actions, lead to negative results. For every event that occurs, there will follow another event whose existence was caused by the first, and this second event will be pleasant or unpleasant according to its cause.

People feel that if something bad happens to them, they must have done something terrible in a past life, and now it's payback time.

Karma is not bad or good. Karma is the basic law of cause-and-effect. The Bible says that what you reap is what you sow, so be mindful of what you sow.

Karma is not in place to punish us; it's there to teach us to live in harmony with the universe. We have no control over Karma, but what we do have control over is the cause that we set in motion and our attitude in dealing with the effect. It is our attitude that makes Karma a positive or negative effect on our lives.

Karma is a natural law. There is no higher instance, no judgment, no divine intervention that steers our destiny—except the law of Karma itself, and it works on a universal scale. Deeds yield consequences—in the next second or in the next hour, day, month, year, decade, or even lifetime.

For example, let's say that you are an individual named John, and you have a plan to overcome excessive spending. But this turns out to be a tall order, so despite your best human efforts, you reach the end of your lifetime without having mastered the lesson. As the human being called John, your soul has made some progress toward overcoming spending. Yet on this lesson, your soul still has work to do. At the end of this lifetime as John, your soul sheds John's physical body, but the energy of the unfinished lesson still exists as a blockage in your soul-level conscious. This energy moves into the body and mind of your next lifetime—as Frank.

As Frank grows up with excessive spending habits. These habits are directly influenced by the unresolved lesson left behind by John. Frank's family is confused by his behavior, and Frank himself doesn't even understand his own actions. Having gone bankrupt again, Frank's friends and family will no longer support him, and he ends up living on the street. *This is Frank's Karma.* If Frank doesn't succeed in this lifetime, then he may decide to come back as Jane—with this Karma still attached.

We deal with cause and effect every hour of our lives. We deal with the effects of other people's actions, but even then we have a choice in how we let other people's actions affect our lives. Remember, we have no control over what other people think or do. They are on their own paths. Don't judge others, as they are following their own destinies.

I am a firm believer that the big choices never determine our lives. Rather, our small, moment-by-moment choices determine our lives. If those small, everyday choices come from a feeling of love and compassion and do no harm, then that's what you are sending out to the universe, and that's what you will get in return. Then your path in your life will move forward with its goals for this lifetime.

If we make a mindful effort to change the way we look at our lives, knowing that we have lived before, our day-to-day responsibilities may not change, but we will suddenly see doors begin to open, and people will come into our lives with messages that we never would have listened to before. All this could lead to new and exciting directions for us. Remember, these opportunities where always there, but because we were blind to the divine energy that flows through everything, we failed to feel and see the subtle forces that move us.

Karma Number

Here is something you might find interesting: how to determine your Karma number. The Karma number is an ancient Vedic or Indian creation.

The Karma number is supposed to tell you about the baggage you are carrying over from your previous lifetime, which is providing you with lessons to learn in this lifetime.

The shortcut to calculating your Karma number is found by taking the number of your day of birth, subtracting 1, and then reducing the result to a single digit, if necessary, through Fadic addition.

For example if you were born July 7, 1969, subtract 1 from the number of your birth day: $7 - 1 = 6$. Your Karma number would be 6. If you were born on May 29, 1999, you would subtract 1 from 29 and then reduce the double digit through Fadic addition, like this: $29 - 1 = 28$; $2 + 8 = 10$, and $1 + 0 = 1$. Thus, your Karma number would be 1.

Karma Number Meanings

Karma number 0: If you reduce to a zero, then it is possible that you are a new soul or one who has cleared up a lot of karmic debt in your past life. The current life is one where you get to start again with a clean slate.

Karma number 1: The lesson of this karma number is learning to be independent. You may start off this life by being very dependent on others, with the life lesson being that you need to stand on your own two feet. This might manifest as spending most of your life single or being very successful but alone.

Karma number 2: The Karma of this life has to do with learning how to get along with others. You may have taken advantage of others in your past life, and now its payback time. You may find yourself saddled with the responsibility of taking care of someone who is dependent on you. You may also have to learn to be less skeptical and to trust your intuition.

Karma number 3: You may have been frivolous, wasteful, and guilty of not taking things seriously enough. You may also have taken credit for someone else's accomplishment or cheated to get to the top somehow. Your lesson in this life is to be balanced, serious, and responsible.

Karma number 4: You may have been lazy in your past life, so in this life you will be asked to fulfill your potential. You may have to work harder than most people just to make a living. Your Karma requires you to be persistent. Great riches are possible if you keep doing the right thing without complaint.

Karma number 5: You may have been an addict, wasteful, or sexually overactive in your past lifetime. Your lesson in this lifetime will be symbolized by situations that necessitate that you work hard and make sacrifices so you can get ahead later. You may also be dealing with health crises that force you to stay on the straight and narrow.

Karma number 6: You are dealing with the Karma of betraying or abandoning your family in a past lifetime. In this lifetime you may find yourself in the position of having to care for your family or take care of someone who is ill. You may also find it hard to strike out on your own and leave the family nest.

Karma number 7: You are dealing with the Karma of failing to pay attention to the spiritual side of your life. You may have been too focused on money in your past life, so in this lifetime it may be more challenging for you to make money. You may be dealing with an illness or chronic problem that also tests your faith.

Karma number 8: You may have been in a position of power and abused it somehow in your past life. It is also possible that you may have exploited others for financial gain. In this life you are doomed to be a follower. You will probably have to get by in this lifetime with less money than most, and you will likely have to work hard to get ahead in life.

Karma number 9: You are dealing with the Karma of avoiding assisting or loving other people in a past life. Your lesson in this lifetime is to learn to be kind and compassionate and to help others. You will probably start this life with great personal needs of your own and will only progress in life after you learn how to be a teacher or a philanthropist in your own life.

CHAPTER 7

Regression

Spontaneous Regression: Déjà Vu

Most of us have had the experience of meeting someone for the first time and feeling as if we have known that person for years, like an old friend. No matter how hard we try to remember where we have met this individual previously, the memory just escapes us.

Déjà vu is the feeling that we have previously witnessed or experienced a currently new situation. In other words, a present moment feels as if it has already happened in the past. Déjà vu is a memory of something that hasn't happened yet or a memory of something that is happening right now.

When you experience déjà vu, it lasts about five seconds. It feels like you had the exact experience before, like you know exactly what is about to happen.

Maybe you have traveled to a new part of the world and have found things to be familiar—like knowing that there is an old school just around the corner. Well, how do you know this kind of thing? It just seems like you have been there before. And maybe you have—in a previous life.

Have you ever gone to a party where you experience an immediate dislike toward someone there—for no apparent reason? Then you wonder why you would dislike someone you don't even know. Maybe you had some previous dealing with this person in a past life and didn't like the outcome.

This happens to most of us on a regular basis, but we usually repress the experience out of fear and lack of understanding.

There have been so many instances in my life where I didn't follow my feelings, especially about people. I would say to myself that I would be crazy not to do business with an individual just because of an unjustified feeling or dislike. On more than one occasion, I ended up getting involved with such people, going against my own feelings. The business situations ended up in total chaos and litigation. My costs were ten times the original profit made by the business deal in the first place.

Follow your feelings. These insights from the past are messages to you or your client. Beware. Learn your lessons from the past, or you will repeat them.

Dreams

The dreams of both children and adults often have bits and pieces of past-life memories. Nightmares and reoccurring dreams may have their bases in some tragic experience from the past.

It's important *not* to actively seek past-life memories from young children. Simply listen to what they say. Consider whether the information provided by the dream explains some unusual patterns, behaviors, or insecurities. Be careful not to traumatize your children by handling unusual situations as behavior problems that call for discipline rather than understanding.

The best thing we can do for our children in relation to possible past-life influences is to listen and observe their behavior with patience.

We can encourage positive behavior and provide opportunities for any possible positive talents to be developed.

We should observe negative or unusual behavior and try to determine if it's normal behavior for a certain age group or a personality trait. When children are relaxed and happy, we can sometimes ask them why they act in a certain way. We must be careful not to judge, criticize, or pry too deep. We do not want to create fear or anxiety within the child.

No matter how wild or strange a fear or concern may be, we must not laugh or belittle it. Our children depend on us for security and safety.

For example, a child who is afraid of the dark and wants to sleep with a night-light on may have been a POW in a dark cell before he died. Another child who is afraid of the water may have drowned in a past life.

Over time, with patience and positive support, they will outgrow their fears.

The New Children

A large percentage of children born after 1988 have blue auras. That's why a lot of researchers call them Indigo children. The reason I am bringing this up is because you are most likely to come across quite a few of these Indigo children through your past-life work.

Humanity is experiencing a leap in evolution. IQ scores throughout the developed world have soared dramatically since tests were introduced in the early twentieth century.

The rise is so sharp that it implies that the average school child today is as bright as the near geniuses of yesteryear. The gene pool cannot change fast enough to account for this jump.

Creative problem-solving has also soared. What are the numbers? Around 30 percent scored between 150 and 160, making the leap in youngsters' intelligence a 24 to 26 point rise from the IQ marker used in past years for scoring geniuses at 134 to 136.

The new children are ultrasensitive to drugs (legal or illegal) and improper nutrition. As a rule, they don't assimilate processed or convenience foods well. These children are unusually psychic and sensitive. Their internal realities are as powerfully real to them as anything in the external world around us.

According to prophecy, today's new children are said to represent an advancement of the human race, which is here to return us to the "natural order." "Natural order" refers to an awareness of the consequences of actions taken, of inner truth, of admitting mistakes and then focusing on who they are deep inside themselves. They know there are no free passes in life. Through a deep understanding gained only through past lives, they operate in the now. They seek solutions to problems rather than obsess over past mistakes. They live totally in-the-moment.

I had an experience with one of my daughter's friends. She was telling my wife about being in the army a long time ago and being shot. My wife told me about this, so the next time the friend came over, my wife suggested that she tell me about her dreams.

My daughter's friend told me that she had been in the army. I asked her what she wore, and she said that she had a big turban wrapped around her head and that she must have been a girl because she was wearing a dress.

I asked her if she had anything to protect herself with. She said she had a big, heavy gun that only shot one bullet at a time. It had a big knife on the front of it.

I asked what else she could tell me, and she said that it was very smoky and hot. Everyone was running and yelling, and she didn't know what to do. Then she got shot in the head and died. She went on to say it was okay, that it hadn't hurt. She hadn't felt a thing.

At this time, I stopped. I really wanted to go further with her after-death experience, but intuitively I knew it was time to stop. I thought she must have been in India, most likely fighting the British.

I tell you this because that is how connected these new Indigo children are to the mind, body, and spirit.

When working with these children, remember that some of them are now in their twenties and that their sensitivity has an emotional as well as intellectual component. Intellectual complexity goes hand-in-hand with emotional depth. Sensitive children not only *think* differently from other children, but they also *feel* differently.

Emotional intensity in sensitive people is not a matter of feeling *more* than other people. It is just a different way of experiencing the world.

Hypnosis

Conventional hypnosis is probably the most widely used method for past-life regression and should be performed by a competent hypnotist who has no prejudice against the theory of reincarnation. The issue is to find a professional hypnotist who believes in reincarnation and has experience in past-life regressions.

The main drawback in using conventional hypnosis is the lack of conscious involvement of the person being regressed. It is possible for the hypnotist to overlook significant clues to the areas that should be more fully explored. Sometimes, through carelessness or overeagerness, questions are asked in a way that suggests answers to the subconscious. It is also possible for the hypnotist to force one's recall into areas of traumatic or embarrassing situations. Often the person being regressed must rely heavily on the hypnotist's own account of the regression rather than their own memory. The hypnotist's version of the regression may be colored by his own interpretations or judgments.

Multi-Level Awareness

This is my preferred choice in past-life regression work. Using the multi-level awareness regression methods presented in this course allows you, the facilitator, to choose the direction of the investigation of a past-life experience. During the regression, the person being regressed can terminate the session at any point and have full recall of the events relived. He can make his own choice about reliving uncomfortable or traumatic experiences. He is in control and can avoid answering questions or can just keep the information for his own use.

With this method, a person learns of all his past lives, all his experiences since creation. This method is done without trance or hypnotic suggestion. This method allows one's consciousness to choose vantage points and look into different planes. It is then possible to see anything in the present or past, to discover why one is here, and to realize, plan for, and execute the real meaning of life.

This technique is not to be taken lightly. It is the start of a mental-spiritual experience.

Soul Knowledge

It's important to have an accurate picture of your soul in order to better understand reincarnation.

One way to find your soul's purpose is through the *akashic records*. *Akashic* is a Sanskrit word meaning "primary substance, that out of which all things are formed."

The akashic records are a dimension of consciousness that contains a vibrational record of every soul and its journey. This vibrational body of consciousness exists everywhere in its entirety and is completely available at all times.

The records are a body of knowledge that contains everything that every soul has ever thought, said, and done over the course of its existence, including all its future possibilities.

The akashic records deal mainly with the soul's purpose for its existence, not necessarily the reincarnation of each lifetime.

CHAPTER 8

Beginning Your Journey

Most people who believe in reincarnation have an inaccurate view of the workings of past-life exploration. Once you start investigating your own past lives, you begin to see things more clearly and experience benefits to your present life.

There is a vast difference between the theory of reincarnation and the actual experience of past-life recall. Those of us who grew up in Western culture have never really considered reincarnation as a truth to be investigated.

When reincarnation does start to surface, perhaps spontaneously to some people—and I am sure this will certainly happen to you—stick with this course, and a world will open up before your eyes.

The place to start is the way you see yourself. Self-knowledge is one of the most difficult things to look for, but it is also one of the most important things we can do for ourselves.

So, if you are ready to begin investigating your past lives, be prepared to undergo some of the strangest emotional experiences of your entire life. These experiences can enrich you, but they can also cause you great emotional pain, and some people are shocked that these memories exist in their minds.

We talked earlier about spontaneous regression. Did you know it is possible to stimulate such memories and that the key to doing so is in your own imagination? In this and the following exercises, I will show you how to use your imagination in a certain way and then analyze the results for past-life clues.

Any conclusions you come up with have to be filed away as unproven, but later you will be able to validate them.

The first thing to do is go out and buy a big notebook. You will be using it throughout the course. In the notebook, write briefly about your own ideas concerning the structure of the mind and your perception of the reincarnation process. Don't spend too much time on it. No one is looking for an essay. A few simple notes will act as a touchstone for you in the months ahead.

Next, try to imagine how would you feel, how would you react, if you were given absolute, conclusive proof that you had lived before. Think about the changes you would make in your life as a result of this knowledge.

What comes next may take a little longer. It's your first step toward awakening far memories. Start by answering this question: if you could win an all-expenses-paid trip to any country in the world, where would you like to go? Imagine you have lots of time off work and that travel will be worry-free with all expenses paid. All you have to do is select your destination. Write your answer in the space provided below.

Once you have written your answer, close your eyes and try to imagine what you would find there. Accuracy is not important. What we are looking for is what you *expect* to find. Make it as wide ranging as possible. Think of the sorts of places you would see, the people you would expect to meet. Think in terms of smells, colors, and music. Try on the architecture, typical furnishings, etc.

Don't rush. Take as much time as you need. At the end of your session, write down your expectations in your notebook under the heading of the country you selected. There is no need to go into fine detail with this record, but make sure to note the important points as memory prompters. When you have done this, complete the questionnaire below:

1. Have you ever read any stories, fact or fiction, about your selected destination? If so, name any you remember that stood out.

_____

_____

_____

_____

2. Do you enjoy watching movies or TV programs about your selected destination? Again, name any that stood out.

_____

_____

_____

_____

_____

3. Do you happen to know anybody from that country? If so, describe your feeling toward them.

---

4. What foods do you associate with your selected destination? Have you ever tasted them?

---

5. List any particularly strong feelings you may have experienced when you were imaging your selected destination.

---

6. Do you have anything in your home—furnishings, rugs, pictures, and so forth—that remind you of your selected destination for any reason? If so, list them.

_____

_____

_____

_____

_____

When you have completed the questionnaire, return to your notebook and take as much time and space as you need to write a fictional account of the sort of person you might have been, had you lived a past life in your selected destination. Make it as detailed as possible, and don't leave anything out. Write about the house you lived in and the clothes you wore. Each and every detail must be from your imagination only.

If you are like most of us, this exercise provokes a feeling of longing for something that you can't put your finger on. Some people report sadness, as if they are missing someone or something.

Others have reported a feeling of excitement, as they are ready to move on to further explore this fascinating area of human existence.

This is the beginning of your exploration. Enjoy the ride.

CHAPTER 9

Frequently Asked Questions about Past-Life Exploration

What is past life exploration?

Past life exploration is a process of self-discovery and spiritual healing. It involves becoming aware of a person's unresolved problems—in a present or past life—that affect their health and quality of life. Past-life regression is a self-guided, efficient method for resolving unconscious patterns contributing to emotional, physical, and behavioral issues.

Past life therapy uses multi-level regression, which can help resolve repressed memories affecting virtually all issues, such as addictions, weight issues, mood disorders, anxieties, and so on. It may resolve fears, traumas, and associated confusion. Release from these behaviors allows the development of one's intuition and shifts the law of attraction. The individual can then attract healthy, loving relationships and can feel inner peace. Past life regression allows a person to face the dark (fear) and bring in the light (inner peace).

What if I can't recall my past lives?

Once in a relaxed state, the mind will gravitate to those issues that most need to be resolved, including the past-life memory affecting your present life today. Everyone can access past memories. What works best is to approach the experience with an open mind, not expecting anything in particular.

Should I have fears about this type of therapy?

You have nothing to fear and everything to gain with past life therapy. The emotional pain of remembering something you did not want to know in a session is much less painful or frightening than a lifetime of unconsciously recreating the same issue over and over again.

What is the unconscious mind?

The unconscious mind records every word, action, and thought. Past-life regression releases harmful recordings; it does not erase the memory. Your emotional behavior changes when these experiences have been brought to light. Many people expect that they are going to see their past lives vividly and in great detail. This isn't always the case, especially when experiencing your first regression. Some clients find that they "see" things in their mind's eye quite clearly. Others may find the impressions somewhat vague, with only portions coming clearly. Information comes through in a number of ways: physical sensations (feeling hot or cold), hearing what people are saying around you, or knowing something intuitively all of a sudden. Just focus on the images and feelings you experience, and don't worry if it makes any sense or not.

Are there any risks in past life regression?

Most people find their experience enlightening, challenging at times, humorous, and life-changing. Many people report increased energy and focus. The trapped feeling in life disappears, and you feel free. Past-life regression accesses the cellular memory and allows for traumas, accidents, and surgeries to be released.

Do I need to believe in reincarnation?

The mind functions beyond currently held beliefs to cause the release and change needed at the deeper level of the mind. A belief in Karma, spirituality, or past lives is not necessary for the treatment to be effective.

Why do people get involved with past-life regression?

Initially, people get involved for self-interest. They want to know who they were in the past, but they quickly realize that there is much more to past-life regression. Your clients will see a direct connection between who they are today and who they were in the past.

Some of the issues that may be helped by past-life regression are: self-esteem, eating disorders, addictions, sleep disorders, focus, fears/phobias, post-traumatic stress, interpersonal skills, anger management, feeling stuck, motivation, inspiration, dream analysis, spiritual growth, and more.

There are some newer areas in which past-life therapy is being applied as well, and they are quite exciting and rewarding. Rather than going after traumatic or troubling memories, they focus on positive experiences. These areas include:

- Accessing strengths and accomplishments from prior lifetimes that can be brought forward to increase confidence and effectiveness in the present

- Re-experiencing a happy, successful lifetime, which can bring a sense of peace when undergoing difficult times and strengthen us to work through our temporary difficulties.

- Clarifying direction and life purpose by viewing one's blueprint for this lifetime.

- Finding prior lifetimes shared with current loved ones, bringing a sense of reassurance that we are indeed never parted from those we love.

- Accessing the wisdom, peace, and guidance that are available to all of us for the "interlife" (spiritual realms between lifetimes), where our guides can access our progress and give direction for our current lifetime.

- Strengthening the clarity of the spiritual nature of our existence.

In compliance with state and federal laws, I note here that past life regression therapy does not claim to diagnose, treat, prevent, or cure diseases. Past-life regression is currently considered alternative therapy and cannot accept insurance payments for services.

CHAPTER 10

Regression Therapy

Psychoanalysis

The process of moving back toward childhood is known by the psychoanalytic term *regression*. In the therapeutic process of regression, it is considered important that these experiences be remembered so vividly that their emotional charge is released, a process known as *abreaction*. Most psychoanalysis is carried out as a therapy in an attempt to relieve a patient's symptoms. The therapist seeks to guide the client toward those forgotten experiences that have a subconscious negative effect.

In the practice of psychoanalysis, the therapist believes that the most troublesome experiences might be the earliest ones. At the moment of birth, for example, you leave the warmth, peace, and security of your mother's womb to plunge into a confusion of light, noise, helplessness, and pain. Such analysts push regression to extremes. Their patients recall cradle events and even the birth trauma itself. Some claim to remember life within the womb. In a few patients, regression produces memories of life before the womb. Initially, these were thought to be some form of hallucinations, which seemed a likely explanation. If the reports of these patients were correct, it would mean that they had actually lived before, and this opened up a whole series of scientific and philosophical difficulties.

Past-life and age regression are fast becoming one of the main keys in therapy. Given the opportunity, the mind will seek solutions to problems. Some believe that remembered past lives are just the result of a vivid imagination. At the very least, these regressions give the individual insight into relationships, causes (whether real or not) of problems, traumas, fears, and phobias. The regression enhances social consciousness and generates tolerance and understanding of all peoples of the world. The individual becomes a more balanced, more complete person. It opens the door to the understanding and shouldering of personal responsibility. It helps people rid themselves of unnecessary and unhealthy guilt feelings. Personal relationships benefit, and deep, fulfilling insight into one's own nature can be gained. The regression experience allows individuals to discover the potentials of their own minds and to gather information and understanding on both practical and spiritual levels.

Self-Responsibility

In regressions, people choose for themselves a role or situation to remember that best meets the needs for the moment. This occurs at the deeper alpha level of the mind for the reliving and release of guilt, fear, and negative feelings. The enhancement of positive feelings and traits has a very real and immediate effect. Another important aspect of this type of regression therapy is that the individual involved is immediately in the position of taking responsibility for himself rather than developing a dependency on the therapist.

The regression experience allows an individual a healthy way to release anger, frustration, and stress—all of which contribute to mental, spiritual, and physical disease. Changes in attitude and life perspective are usually generated by the regression experience, and patients often find that there are fewer times in the future that initiate anger, frustration, and stress. Individuals become more relaxed in life, thereby producing a healthier mental and emotional state.

A number of therapists who use hypnosis for age regression in search of the causative factors of problems have found themselves in situations where they are directing patients to return to the source of their problems—and then the patients regress to a past life, when neither therapist nor patient had ever considered the possibility of reincarnation. Those who continue to discount the possibility of reincarnation after such an experience often offer the explanation that, if a situation in life is painful, distressing, or embarrassing, it may be easier for an individual to detach himself from his present life and move into the fantasy of a past life. Whatever explanation one chooses to use, the past-life regression experience does give the individual the courage to understand and deal with problems that otherwise might be avoided. If it brings about positive results, with a happier, healthier, and more productive individual as the end result, then it seems to be a tragic waste not to use past-life regression as a therapeutic tool—whatever a person's belief about reincarnation.

Drugs and Alcohol

There are so many areas in which little or no work has been done to explore the practical applications of past-life regression. The future holds exciting possibilities for those with enough foresight to undertake such research, especially considering the positive results of using past-life regression to explore and understand the underlying causes of drug and alcohol addiction in some individuals. Past-life regression has the potential for being an important tool in understanding what factors contribute to an addictive makeup. Though little work has been done in this area, a significant enough percentage of addicted individuals have found permanent relief through regression to make it worthwhile to investigate. It is not enough that an individual develops self-control to avoid drugs and alcohol. A person has the right to find ways to eliminate mental factors that cause the craving. Such help should not be denied to anyone on the basis of philosophical differences or religious or scientific prejudices.

Preventive Therapy

The use of regression offers an open door to the possibility of understanding and eliminating the causes of many of the ills of our society. For example, if solid information could be compiled regarding underlying past-life factors that may cause some people to commit acts of violence—while others with the same background in the present lifetime who are thrust into the same situations do not—there is a strong probability that potentially violent individuals could be recognized early in life and defused through past-life regression.

Past-life regression, however, must never be allowed to become an excuse for avoiding responsibility for such actions. We are each responsible for our actions and must accept the consequences of those actions. Prevention is the answer.

Since the psychological makeup of a person often plays an important role in illness and accidents, it seems that there is a place here also for the use of past-life regression. The possible past-life influences in attitudes toward food—which cause underweight or overweight problems—are worth looking into. There have also been some cases where the beginnings of allergies have been traced to past-life situations. The vast scope of possible past-life benefits is limited only by our imagination. This is not to suggest that past-life regression will answer the world's problems, but there are many answers to be found in the process. I can see in the future where past-life regression may become as much a rite of passage into adulthood as puberty. Many potential problems could be eliminated before they become handicaps, and positive attitudes could be reinforced.

Reincarnation Investigation

There are two ways you can carry out reincarnation investigations, on other people or on yourself. Using other people is certainly interesting and sometimes fascinating, but as you began to find out earlier in the book, there is nothing to beat finding out who you used to be. Once you begin to understand the mechanics of reincarnation, you come to realize that the information is all locked up in the deeper parts of your mind. Your only real problem is reaching it. Your practical work with creative fantasy does not produce something out of nothing. Rather, it looks for raw material and reworks it or just dusts it off and reprints it. By allowing your mind to roam freely, you open the door to many different channels through which information might potentially flow. Whether or not the material you have already recorded in your notebook represents genuine past-life recall is something you will have to investigate at a later date. For the time being, it is enough to gather and record clues.

Relaxation Technique

Your main task for this lesson is similar in many ways to the exercise you carried out in your notebook. But before we come to it, we want to add a technique that will not only help you with this lesson's exercise but will be increasingly important to you as you move through the reminder of the course. Starting tomorrow morning and continuing each morning thereafter, we ask that you set aside a short period for the practice of relaxation. How much time you spend is up to you. You will find that anything less than ten minutes is not worthwhile, and we do not want you to spend more than half an hour, unless you are experienced in the art.

You will need privacy. This is one reason for selecting a morning time. If you get up early enough, nobody else will be about. Try to find a place where you will not be disturbed by people, pets, or ringing phones. Lock the door if you need to. If you are sensitive to noise, use earplugs.

Conduct your relaxation session in an upright chair. Do not lie down on a couch or bed to keep from falling asleep. Begin by regulating your breathing. Relaxation is a physical function. Your muscles use oxygen extracted from your bloodstream. Your bloodstream, in turn, extracts that oxygen from the air you breathe. By regulating your breathing, you increase the oxygen available in your blood. Your muscles extract the optimum amount and are far happier to relax for you than they might be otherwise.

If you have studied yoga, you will know that there are all sorts of complex breath-regulation techniques. The one we want you to try is very simple. It's called 2/4 breathing:

1. Breath in to the mental count of four.

2. Hold your breath in to the mental count of two.

3. Breathe out to the mental count of four.

4. Hold your breath out to the mental count of two.

It sounds simple, and it is, although you should be warned that there is a knack for getting it right. You will know when you have right, when you begin doing it without thinking. The rate at which you count varies from person to person. Get your breathing right before you go on to the second part of this exercise. It is okay for you to devote an entire session—or a whole year of sessions—to getting your breathing comfortable.

Once you establish a comfortable rhythm of 2/4 breathing, let it run for about three minutes. Then start the following relaxation sequence. If you can hold the 2/4 rhythm while you do it, that's great, but you may not succeed at first. In that case, just start your session with three minutes of 2/4 breathing, and then go back to normal breathing while you carry out the main relaxation sequence. Then, take up 2/4 breathing again when you are relaxed. Here is the relaxation sequence.

1. Concentrate on your feet. Wiggle them about. Curl them to tense the muscles, and then allow them to relax.

2. Concentrate next on your calf muscles. Tighten and relax them.

3. Concentrate on your thigh muscles. Tighten and relax them.

4. Concentrate on your buttock muscles. Tighten and relax.

5. Concentrate on your stomach muscles, a common tension focus. Tighten and then relax them.

6. Concentrate on your hands. Curl them to make fists and then relax them.

7. Concentrate on your arms. Tighten them rigidly and then relax them.

8. Concentrate on your back. Tighten the muscles and then relax them.

9. Concentrate on your chest. Tighten the muscles and then relax them.

10. Concentrate on your shoulders, another common tension focus. Hunch your shoulders to tighten the muscles, and then relax them.

11. Concentrate on your neck. Tighten the muscles, then relax.

12. Concentrate on your face. Grit your teeth and contort your features to tense up the facial muscles, and then relax them.

13. Concentrate on your scalp. Tighten the scalp muscles, then relax them.

14. Now tighten up every muscle in your body, holding your entire body rigid momentarily. Then relax, letting go as completely as you are able. Do this final whole-body sequence again—three times in all. On the third time, take a really deep breath when you tense the muscles, and then sigh deeply as loud as you can as you let the tension go.

15. You should be feeling relaxed by now. If you stopped your 2/4 breathing at the start of the relaxation sequence, pick it up again at this point.

16. Close your eyes and try to imagine your whole body getting heavier and heavier, as if it was turning to lead. You will find your visualization increases your level of relaxation still further.

Enjoy the sensation of relaxation for the reminder of your session, but stay vigilant. Should you find tension creeping in anywhere (and you will in the early days) don't let it worry you. Just tighten up the tense muscles a little more, and then relax them. It is important to start regular daily practice. You should be feeling some benefit inside of a week, and you may be quite proficient within two weeks. Use the technique regularly until you train yourself to relax totally anytime, anywhere. This may take several months, but don't let that worry you. The important thing is that you have made a start and are determined to continue practicing the technique until you are proficient.

Once you have started on conscious relaxation, you can start in on your next memory stimulation exercise, which covers something ignored in lesson 2. In that lesson, you were invited to search for past-life memories anywhere in the world. But you probably never dreamed of looking right here at home. Past lives are not always located in some exotic foreign land. The possibility arises that you have reincarnated more than once in the same country. You should consider that possibility now. Go through your relaxation exercise until all tensions have been released, and then answer this question: what county, village, town, city, or other location of your native country would you like to visit?

The term *native country* should be taken to mean the country in which you are living now (or have lived most of your life) and not necessarily the country where you were actually born. Your selected location may be a place you have already visited or somewhere you have never been before. When you have made your choice, complete the questionnaire below.

Questionnaire

1. What feelings, positive or negative, do you experience when you think of that part of your country?

_____

_____

_____

_____

_____

2. If you have not already visited this area, what would you expect to find there? Allow your mind to roam freely so that it is not confined to things about the district you already live in.

_____

_____

_____

_____

_____

3. Do you associate a certain type of person with this area? If so, what are your feelings, positive or negative, toward that sort of person?

_____

_____

_____

_____

_____

4. When you have filled in your answers, turn back to your notebook. Imagine yourself actually visiting your selected location for the first time or for a return trip. As you visit, imagine that some object, sight, or experience triggers a memory of a past life.

_____

_____

_____

_____

_____

CHAPTER 11

Regression: A Method for Change

All souls were created at the same time, yet the world's population fluctuates drastically. Even now, our present population is greater than at any other time in history. What's happening to all the souls? Part of the answer is that not all souls incarnate at the same time. When a particular world situation offers a large scope of opportunity for experiences and a great potential for spiritual development, more souls incarnate than at any other time. Souls that are not incarnated are not dormant. They have their periods of learning and growth in nonphysical planes of existence, where time as we measure it in the physical world does not exist. While they are learning on those planes, they are also watching and waiting for the optimum conditions for further experience in the physical plane to occur.

It must also be noted that estimates of the world population in the past are not necessarily accurate. They do not take into consideration any evidence that may support the probable existence of highly technological societies that may have destroyed themselves in the far past. Even if one discounts the stories of Atlantis and ancient civilizations inside the Gobi Desert, one must take into consideration the fact that modern humans are not always as knowledgeable about things as we originally thought.

As time moves on, we are becoming increasingly aware of things we have previously taken for granted. Historical accounts are all being rewritten and proven false. For example, we once took it as absolute truth that modern man has existed for about forty thousand years. Then we discovered a skull of modern man that dates back over four hundred thousand years. There is strong archaeological evidence that modern man may have developed here in North America and then migrated to other parts of the planet, rather than the reverse.

Not so many years ago, an atom was defined as the smallest indivisible particle of matter. School children now know about protons, neutrons, electrons, and a myriad of facts about the structure of the atom. We were taught that the first European landing and settlement in North America was in Jamestown. Now we know that St. Augustine was a thriving town in the late fifteenth century.

For all that man has learned and accomplished, we are still wondering about where we came from. Did we evolve, or were we created? Or was it a combination of both? Was the universe created, or did it happen with a big bang? Is it expanding or shrinking? Is the planet headed toward an ice age, or is it getting hotter? Why did the dinosaur disappear? You can hear a hundred theories presented as fact.

Even the facts we think we know, about yesterday or thousands or millions of years ago, are open to interpretation and change. Already we know that many civilizations have existed in the past, and many have vanished without a trace.

A significant fact from all of this is that there are more souls incarnated at the present time than during any known historical period, indicating that the opportunities offered for growth of the soul are huge. Because of the strength of our numbers, we have the potential for making vast, far-reaching changes in our world. We have made terrible mistakes, which could destroy our present environment and negate all of our technological advances. Sometime in the distant future, we could become one of those lost civilizations whose very existence is considered a fable. Or we can make a decision to use our potential to remember and understand past errors in judgment and action, and refuse to repeat the destructive cycles.

Personal Responsibility

We are each personally responsible for the role we play in the destiny of our civilization. We must be willing to take the time and make the effort to understand our past lives, not just as they relate to our present, individual selves but in how our actions and attitudes contribute to the rise and fall of the civilizations we live in. After the initial experiences of exploring past lives and coming to a better understanding of ourselves, we need to take a long, hard look at the social consciousness we exhibited in past lives and ask ourselves some questions.

Were there lifetimes in which we thought of ourselves as superior to others and set ourselves above others? Did we believe that people didn't have the intellectual capacity to decide their own everyday aspects of life for themselves, that we had to tell them how to dress, what to be, what to think, how to raise their children, how to worship god, and which god to worship? Did we tell them and ourselves that, for their own good, we must limit personal freedom of choice? Did we do that or allow it to be done to us?

If you think about it, that's going on in our culture today. The government is getting so large and powerful that it is basically trying to control the people, from the foods we eat to the doctors we can see. It is spending money we don't have, with 40 percent being thrown away on ridiculous programs and waste, leading us into bankruptcy. At this moment, the United States is almost seventy trillion dollars in the hole, not counting future liabilities. We plow under our farmland and are now net importers of food. We were once the breadbasket of the world, and now we can't even feed ourselves.

Did we decide that any political beliefs different from our own were wrong, that any religious beliefs different from our own were in error, or that any social or cultural practice different from our own was inferior? Did we feel that those differences gave us the right to apply force or even death to bring people into line with our opinion of what was right? Did we try to force our beliefs on those around us, blocking the possibility of peaceful discussion that might bring about increased knowledge, understanding, and tolerance on all sides? Were their lifetimes in which we allowed ourselves to be lazy and indifferent, as personal freedoms slipped away, one by one? Each change may have seemed small, not having much effect on our personal lives at the time. Perhaps the changes bothered us a little, but we pacified ourselves by thinking that someone else would speak up and do something—and then one day it was too late.

Isn't that what is going on today in our world? Look around us! The governments of the world try to control everything and everybody. We need to speak up now! Big government has an agenda that is designed to force us to depend on it. Government wants to remove everything we may rely on for mental and spiritual support.

Consider this:

- 93 percent want "in God we trust" to be left on our currency
- 93 percent celebrate Christmas
- 97 percent are not offended by "Merry Christmas"
- 90 percent support keeping "God" in our pledge of allegiance
- 87 percent want our religious holidays left on the public school calendars
- 84 percent support references to God in our public buildings
- 83 percent support the display of nativity scenes
- 82 percent support voluntary school prayer
- 76 percent support the Ten Commandments displays on public property

But all of the above are slowly being taken away from us, as we sit by and watch it happen. These are times when we have to stand up and defend principles, but we are afraid. Within each of us is the capacity to bring the voice of reason to a situation, to bring the one voice that might help convince others to take action to change things. In past lives, did we remain silent? When other people raised voices of reason and warned of the course of the future, did we listen and take action, or did we tell ourselves, "It can't happen here"?

These are some examples of things that have happened in the past and are happening today. Big government has silenced most people with three simple accusations: "You're racist, you're intolerant, and you don't care about the poor." These have made our world a place where the truth does not matter anymore, where being politically correct is the only way for society to act.

This is being furthered by big media, which constantly bombards us with lies. It tells teenage girls that they are somewhat inadequate if they don't look like Christine Aguilera, Brittany Spears, or Lindsay Lohan. If you are a man, you're told that you are not looking after yourself or your family if you are not driving an expensive car and living in a four-thousand-square-foot home with a pool. The media has taken our personal sense of identity away from us.

Great civilizations and empires have risen and fallen. Where are the great Roman, Persian, and Ottoman empires, or the Aztecs and Mayans, to name a few? It is the nature of such political and cultural structures that they rise to greatness, and then, when they seem almost invincible, they decline into internal decay. Isn't that what is happening in the United States today?

Government is trying to make more and more of the population dependent on some form of government handout. Parties win elections based on who is going to give the most freebies to the people. Meanwhile, they are taking resources from those who work hard and look after themselves. At Rome's greatest time of prosperity, Caesar decided to give the beggars on the street one meal a day. Within no time, the population of beggars grew by leaps and bounds.

At that time, immigrants from conquered lands demanded to be Roman soldiers, but a person had to be Roman to be a soldier. Eventually, through mounting pressure from the conquered lands, Caesar allowed a change in policy—in spite of the Roman peoples' wishes to the contrary. Within a short period of time, soldiers started to turn on each other. Combined with moral decay and high taxes to pay for the handouts, this eventually lead to the destruction of Rome. Rome collapsed from the inside out—which is exactly what is happening in the United States today. Of course, Rome didn't collapsed in just a few months, but over time, the burdens became too much for Rome to bear. Conquered countries started to break away, and Rome no longer had the power to stop them.

You might be wondering what this has to do with past-life research.

Well, if you believe in reincarnation and take the time to consider your past lives on a broader scale, then you must inevitably find that somewhere, sometime, you played varying roles in the building and destruction of nations. It will also become evident that neither an individual nor a small group of men ever charts the course of history. Whatever great numbers of ordinary citizens allow a few to do is what writes the pages of history.

Examine the social structures of times and places where you have lived past lifetimes, and the roles you played. Look at the world around you and compare those memories with your attitudes and roles today. Ask yourself the same questions about today that you have asked yourself about the many yesterdays. Allow what is good, strong, and constructive to be fully integrated into your present self. Leave behind those attitudes that were destructive and caused conflict, but remember them so that you do not make the same errors again.

The world is shaped by our present action or inaction, which will be inherited, not only by our children and grandchildren but by us in our future lifetimes. The problems and negative situations that we have to deal with now are the collective effects of all our past-life actions.

How often it has been said that the tragedy of the human race is that it never learns from the past. We must learn from the past about accepting personal responsibility and demanding responsible action from those who lead our nations.

It has been human nature to jump on the bandwagon for anything to do with new technology. We must learn from the past and be more selective about what we are willing to accept. For example, if there are potential negative side effects to any new technology, we must ensure that we find a way to deal with those side effects before that new technology is implemented. If such a responsible course of action had been demanded in the past, we would not have a present problem with pollution, nuclear waste, and highly processed foods that are killing our bodies.

Responsible Progress

We must be willing to ask ourselves whether the advantages we gain through progress outweigh the long-term disadvantages. Responsible technological advancement is a boon to all mankind, but the giving of help comes in both responsible and irresponsible forms. We may feed a starving person or provide social welfare programs for the poor, but this doesn't solve the cause of the problem. It creates dependency on the help to the point where people can no longer help themselves. There is an often-quoted Chinese proverb that says, "Give a man a fish and you feed him for a day. Teach a man to fish and you feed him for a lifetime."

True help must meet the present need, but the major part of that help should equip a person with the tools or knowledge to help himself solve or avoid situations that brought about the need in the first place. Knowing your past lives opens your mind to better ways to improve yourself and mankind as a whole.

The past is full of examples that teach us this: if we allow ourselves to fall into the trap of solving another's problems, those problems or similar ones tend to recur in that person's life. He needs to solve his own problems. Then he learns how to deal with situations in the present and in the future.

The past should teach us several things about helping others. If a person really wants to solve a problem, he will find a way. Sometimes the best help we can give another person is *no* help.

Help sometime creates a dependency that can lead to unexpected results. The giver may initially feel a sense of satisfaction or an ego boost, but the recipient's continued dependency usually results in resentment, anger, and rejection. The recipient of the help usually feels an immediate relief and then a sense of helplessness. Often, people trapped in this receiving lifestyle develop the attitude that the world owes them help for the rest of their lives. In truth, the world owes us nothing.

If enough people use past-life regression to know themselves and thereby know and understand their fellow man, they will understand the mistakes of the past and refuse to repeat them. Then there is a chance that the world can be inhabited by tolerant, responsible, peaceful human beings. This can become the age when man finally learns from the past. Then we can turn our thoughts and energies away from wondering whether our world will be destroyed by a nuclear holocaust or wiped out by famine or disease. We can concentrate on the reason for our continued presence in the reincarnation cycle by remembering who, what, where, and how to return to where we have come.

Exercise

In your course notebook, list those areas of your life where you think reincarnation may have had the most influence on you. We understand that you do not know at this stage, and you are not being asked to find out. What you are being asked to do is to think about your life, reviewing your career, your talents, and your phobias with special emphasis on any recurring patterns you find. Then write down those areas where you think reincarnation may have played a role. Writing down your guesses is the easy part. The hard part is the self-examination that will follow. Don't rush this.

It's important. Take as much time as necessary. Once you have done this, you can move on to the next exercise, which is designed to stimulate your far memory. Try it immediately following your relaxation technique.

In this exercise, you are required to imagine yourself entering a very special kind of clothing store. It is a store that carries on its racks clothing from every country in the world. Even as you enter this store, the displayed variety of choice is unbelievable, for you quickly note that not only is every *country* represented but various *periods of time* as well. Here is a panorama of fashion through the ages. As you stand there, a clerk comes up to you, treating you as if you are his best client. You have been given unlimited credit to spend this store.

The clerk says he has just the thing for you. He leads you into a dressing room with a full-length mirror and a wardrobe selected just for you. Look at the clothes carefully, and then put them on and look at yourself in the mirror. With the clothes on, take time to answer the following questions:

1. Describe your costume in your notebook. If you know what country or time period it came from, record that as well. If not, simply describe the style and material in detail. Draw an illustration if you have artistic talent.

_____

_____

_____

_____

_____

2. Make a note of how you felt the first moment you saw the costume.

_____

_____

_____

_____

_____

3. How did you feel immediately after you put it on?

_____

_____

_____

_____

_____

4. Describe how you looked while wearing the costume. Did you notice any unexplained changes in your physical appearance, such as hair color or style, build, facial characteristics, and so on?

_____

_____

_____

_____

_____

5. While you wore the costume, were you aware of any mood changes in yourself, any particular emotions, feelings, or attitudes? If so, describe what they were.

_____

_____

_____

_____

_____

6. Can you spot any linkage between the way the costume made you feel and your current reactions? If so, list them.

_____

_____

_____

_____

_____

Once you have completed this exercise, go on to the next lesson. It will introduce you to a more advanced and very dramatic aspect of reincarnation research.

CHAPTER 12

Past-Life Influence

The possibility that your past life may have made you wiser, more peaceful, and more forgiving may be of little interest to you in this life. But your series of past lives is of great interest. There is a lot of evidence that the way you are now—the way you think and react, the whole pattern of your life—may be profoundly influenced by the way you were. It is human nature to put aside things we don't like or want to remember. Most adults feel that their school days were the happiest of their lives, despite the fact that, in most cases, they were the exact opposite. Older people in particular remember the summers of their childhood as being warmer and drier than they are now, despite the fact that weather in general hasn't changed much over the last fifty years. They are exercising selective memory, a tendency to remember the good times while forgetting the bad. This tendency is actually a protection mechanism. It prevents our minds from being overwhelmed by a series of personal disasters that form part of any normal life. But it is a mechanism that is seriously flawed, because it sometimes works too well.

Psychology—and in particular psychiatry—has taught us how certain experiences can set a pattern for an entire lifetime. The classic example is the sexually abused child who later experiences difficulties in relationships with the opposite sex, perhaps for the rest of his life. But it now seems that our formative years extend beyond childhood into a whole chain of childhoods, not to mention the adult experiences that follow them. The results of their influence vary from the minor to the overwhelming.

Past lives are rarely so intense that they affect our existence the next time around. Researcher Dr. Helen Wambach put it bluntly: going back into your past lives is like going back to your sophomore year in high school. How many more times do you want to remember your gym teacher? Most past lives are pretty boring. Living in interesting times is usually characterized by bloodshed, pain, and trauma. These interesting times leave their psychological mark. Boring lifetimes have little influence on your present lifetime, but every lifetime has at least some influence, often by way of a personality quick, a habit, or even a phobia.

The findings of modern psychology make it easy for us to understand that the mechanics of reincarnation influence present personality. If we know that being locked up in a closet during childhood led to claustrophobia in adulthood, then it really doesn't matter whether that childhood was in this lifetime or another. Sometimes it's hard to understand the mechanics that lead to the repeating of physical illnesses from one lifetime to another. Whatever mechanics are involved in the transfer of physical trauma from one life to another, the actuality of such transfer seems to be uncommonly widespread. It is all too easy to begin to view the reincarnation process as a combination of bad news that creates physical, emotional, and mental problems.

But such a view is totally wrong. Reincarnation is just part of the evolutionary process and, as such, has a mixture of good and bad, pleasure and pain. While you may look for the cause of an illness in past lives, you may also find that your present talents begin to grow there too. There seem to be two types of talents: innate and trained. But even innate talents are improved by practice, and given a bit of determination, many new talents can actually develop the same way. What you are today is a result of what you were before, and that includes your talents instituted and skills professed.

Regression and reincarnation research is a serious business—with possible dangers, once you go beyond a certain state. We have to make sure you understand this point. We would not have presented this course if we did not believe that the potential gains through reincarnation research far outweigh the risks.

How dangerous can regression be? What is the worst that could happen? Although we have never encountered it in our work, medical doctors inform us that the worst that could theoretically happen is death. Multi-level awareness, hypnosis, and any other common regression techniques are not dangerous in themselves. The degree of relaxation possible is usually considered therapeutic, but vivid dramatic experiences could have an adverse effect on certain preexisting physical conditions.

If you have a serious heart condition or any other illness, and a doctor advises that you avoid stress, and you remember that you may have lived during the Civil War, where you watched your friends or yourself being murdered, then being regressed may not be the best thing for your heart. But for most people, the experience of past lives is not remembering; it's reliving. As such, the experience takes almost as much a toll on the body—and just as much a toll on the emotions—as did the original experience.

A good rule of thumb to remember is this: if you're not fit enough to take the exercise in reality, you would be well-advised to keep well away from it in regression. The trouble with this advice is that you often have no hint of what you are going to experience until you're actually in it. But any risks can be minimized. Here are two fundamental safety rules about regression.

1. If you suffer from any physical condition in which stress is a life-threatening factor, do not permit yourself to become the subject of past-life regression under any circumstances.

2. If you decide to do it anyway, make sure the facilitator is aware of your condition and has been told to cut short any past-life experience that causes undue stress.

Those are the basics. Following rule number one should keep you well out of trouble. We recommend that you make it a personal rule never to regress any subject with a heart condition or similar illness.

Persons being regressed are vulnerable to the emotional and mental attitudes of those around them. Every effort should be made to keep the atmosphere positive and light. A healthy sense of humor is not out of place and will often help ease tensions. This is an experiment in recalling memories from the far past. Just as it is easier for some people to recall detailed memories from early childhood, some patients will be able to recall memories from other lifetimes.

Regression subjects open themselves up to experiencing emotional pain, because there's a human tendency to focus on the dramatic. This is not always a bad thing. Doctors treating soldiers learned that the only real cure was to persuade patients to remember the original trauma and relive it along with the conscious discharge of all associated emotions. One popular perception is that confession is good for the soul, but most doctors now agree this is by no means a universal truth. If a person is unable to cope effectively with trauma in his life, he will be no different when it comes to coping with trauma in another.

Past-life regression is, by its very nature, a process of psychoanalysis that involves gaining knowledge about oneself that has been buried deep inside one's memories. Some of this truth may prove to be therapeutic. The bottom line is simply this: a person runs the same emotional risk in regression that he does in psychoanalysis.

The world of past-life regression and reincarnation beliefs includes people who go through life claiming to have been Egyptian pharaohs, Roman generals, or the great talents of their country. I'm sorry to disappoint you, but such claims are usually based on flimsy evidence or no evidence at all. What is at work here is nothing more than wishful thinking, a desire to compensate for shortcomings in this life by claiming an impressive past.

We're not suggesting that people purposely make up their past-life credentials. However, we humans are intrigued and flattered by the possibility that we were once very powerful, rich, talented, or famous. This kind of connection may be exactly the sort of news that certain people desperately need to hear to compensate for their perceived shortcomings in this lifetime. In some circumstances, it is all too easy to become a little sloppy and accept the sort of evidence that might otherwise be rejected. The techniques of reincarnation research are generally valid, but their parallel with psychoanalysis is close. During analysis, it is not unknown for a patient to create a fantasy and to present material that shows his life, not in the way it was but in the way it might have been or should have been.

The same thing may occur in regression experiences. In many cases, the fantasies are constructed with such skill that they are extremely difficult to tell from reality. This is why we stress research. Check to ensure that your facts are correct. Be aware of a fundamental truth: the more flattering a past-life is, the less likely it is to be true. All past-life memories should be checked. Historical personalities will always fall into this category. It is not impossible that you were once George Washington, Alexander the Great, or Shakespeare, but it is highly unlikely.

Unfortunately, the danger of self-deception does not end with well-known historical figures. A quiet introvert might make up a story of a past life as a warrior to make up for his shortcomings in today's world. You must be very careful not to do the same. You want to make sure that your far memories are real. To do so requires self-knowledge and a real understanding of what makes you tick. Dismiss anything for which there is not substantial evidence.

A common question is this: why do people who remember their past lives seem to remember exciting lives rather than dreary existences as farmers or maids? Far too many reincarnation believers like to remind others about their own exciting past lives. Realistically, we must remember three things about memories of past lives.

1. Most people's past lives were anything but glamorous. They were more often mundane existences. The complete picture of a past life may be confused by the appearance of a dramatic incident such as death by fire, drowning, or whatever. But a dramatic incident does not necessary mean a dramatic life.

2. Some past lives are truly dramatic and romantic, just as some present lives are dramatic and romantic. There are people today who climb a mountain or fly to the moon—not many of them, but they do exist. There have always been people who led adventurous lives. Far memory of such a life may be unusual, but it is not impossible.

3. Less obvious is the fact that old memories tend to be remembered as part of a better time and place. You might, for example, find it exciting to learn that you once lived as a Roman legionnaire. Would you be equally impressed if I told you that I had just become a private in the US army? Probability not, but the careers are the same. The only difference is that the Roman army existed earlier in history.

There is only one way to protect yourself from self-deception about reincarnation, and that is to increase your level of self-awareness until you are familiar with your deepest motivations. This is a good place to start.

By now you should have established your daily relaxation routine. Your task for this lesson is to build on your relaxation routine, to change it in essence from simple relaxation to meditation. A great deal of mystery surrounds the practice of meditation, but it's as basic to us as breathing.

Starting tomorrow and continuing on a regular basis thereafter, add ten minutes or so to your morning relaxation regime. When you are totally relaxed and have returned to your 2/4 breathing, you should turn your attention inward. Review everything that happened the previous day.

If you lead a busy life, this may sound like it requires a lot of time, but the trick is not to spend too much time on any one aspect. It is certainly not beneficial to begin fighting old battles or obsessing about what might have been. Simply move systematically from one part of your day to the next, carefully examining your motives for your actions at each point. This is actually the hard part. As you gain proficiency, you will find that remembering is easy, but determining your own motivations will always be tricky. The more skilled you are in the art, the more you will find that the experience becomes increasingly subtle.

The trick is to be totally honest with yourself. Remember that the only person who will ever know your findings is you. Don't even try to write them down. Only observe what it is that makes you act the way you do.

If you find that your mind is starting to wander during your meditation session, simply bring the memories back, and this time write down the problem in your notebook. Don't make a big deal about it. Your complete entry might read:

Meditation: Wednesday, October 15

Start: 7:00 a.m.

Finish: 7:15 a.m.

Mind wandering: 4

Noise interruption: 6

Other breaks in concentration: 2

The purpose of this little record is twofold. It will remind you how often you have found some excuse to avoid meditation, as you certainly will, sooner or later. It will provide an ongoing indicator of progress in the years ahead. As you become more proficient, you will definitely find that mind-wandering and other interruptions become few and far between, compared to the level of frequency when you first began.

If you should find, for any reason, that you really do have to miss a morning meditation, make sure to note that in your notebook too. Your entry can be as simple as: "Meditation: Wednesday, December 6, no meditation, sick."

A few minutes spent each morning in nonjudgmental meditation about your motivations can go a long way toward laying the foundations to true self-knowledge. This will certainly help you in your evaluation of regression and reincarnation research material, and it may prove helpful in others aspects of your life as well.

CHAPTER 13

Preparation for the Regression

When getting ready for your first regression, it is important to find a place where you are going to feel comfortable without worrying about possible interruptions. Later, when you are comfortable with the idea of regression and have gained some expertise in the area, you can regress yourself almost anywhere—with the television going, kids playing, or the telephone ringing. But that's for later. For now, choose a quiet place where you won't be interrupted.

For your first regression you may be more comfortable working with a minimum of three people, one of whom is the reincarnation subject. Make sure that you feel completely comfortable with the people present to conduct your first regression. Regression can be conducted with as many people as you wish. Remember that past-life regressions are not party games and should not be done in a party atmosphere.

Records

Keeping records is an important part of a regression. A complete recording of the regression is great, but written records may be necessary. It is easier to pick out important bits of information from written material than from listening to a recording. At first, written records are only really practical if there is a third person present to take notes. Trying to learn the technique for conducting a regression while trying to take notes at the same time is next to impossible.

If you are taking notes, just writing down the answer will often be enough to tell what the question was. If not, include a few key words so the reader will understand the question later. If you don't understand what the person being regressed has said, ask him to repeat himself. Some people become self-conscious in the present of tape recorders. Use a recorder if it doesn't disturb the regression. Make sure the quality of the recording is the best you can afford; nothing is more frustrating than an interesting regression accompanied by an inaudible recording. If you choose, you can have someone transcribe the recording into a written record. Information that doesn't seem significant at the time can often prove to be important later. Maybe later regressions, when reviewed with earlier recordings, will point to trends or patterns that were not evident at first. After a regression, you will remember a lot more than you verbalized. Those additional details will add a lot more meaning to the regression.

General Instructions for the Person Directing the Regression

Keep a positive, relaxed attitude. Conducting regressions is a learning experience for you that can be used in your own regression. Also, the more expertise you gain in conducting regressions, the better you will be at asking questions and eliciting important information. Remember that this is not a right or wrong situation for either of you. It will not matter if you don't have perfect technique or you ask the wrong questions. This is part of learning the process.

Watch carefully during the regression. Watch for signs of stress or tension: agitated hand movements or tightly clenched fists, clenched jaw, abnormal or uncontrolled laughter, or tears combined with any other signs. Tears alone are not necessarily something to be concerned about, as they are often a healthy release. If you should be faced with a situation where the person being regressed is obviously in great distress, calmly ask if there is anything bothering them and if they would prefer to end the regression or skip that event and go on to something else. Calmly remind them that they are here and now. Tell them that this is simply an exercise in remembering and that there is no need for them to experience any pain or distress of any kind.

If the regressing person tells you that he would prefer to end the regression, repeat positive statements at the end of each regression. If he wants to continue, simply give instructions to progress to a time—a week, month, year, or whatever span of time seems appropriate—*after* that incident, and then proceed. After the regression, it may be a good idea to discuss whatever was causing them distress—if the person wants to do so. The memory will already have been triggered, and often it is easier to discuss and deal with it outside of the regression with less emotional involvement. Be sympathetic and nonjudgmental at all times. Let the person know that discussing the cause of the distress will release the emotions involved and will put the memory into perspective and make it easier to deal with. But don't insist.

You will never have a situation that develops into a traumatic experience if you handle it in this manner. Seldom, if ever, will you encounter a situation of undue distress in a regression experience. You cannot regress a person into a past-life situation where he gets trapped and cannot return to the present time and place. But regression technique is structured in such a way as to have some built-in safeguards. The most important part of regression technique is the emphasis on it being an exercise in remembering—while living in the here and now. The positive closing statements are really beneficial for the person being regressed.

While you are conducting a regression, accept whatever answers are given to your questions. Do not question or argue with the answers. This is not what a facilitator does. Also, be careful that you do not ask leading questions, even if you have impressions of what the person regressing is experiencing. For instance, if the person is not getting clear impressions about their surroundings but you are, do not ask, "Are you in a house?" Rather, ask a question that gives a choice: "Are you inside some structure, or are you outdoors?" Give the person a choice, and his mind will focus on the right answer.

Keep the person observing and conversing. Don't let them get bogged down in fine detail. Lifetimes will provide more detail after a couple of regression experiences, and then the person will feel right at home with the process.

The first regression experience should last approximately one hour. Later regressions may be longer, if necessary. The passage of time is distorted at the particular levels of the mind where you are working. The session may seem longer or shorter than it actually is. In conducting a regression, your function is to assist in focusing attention by asking questions, not to assume control of the person or the session. Conducting a regression is easy. You deal with many more difficult situations every day. It's normal at first to be a little tense, as with any new situation, but the more relaxed you are, the more relaxed the person being regressed will be. People fear the unknown, and the mind is one of the great frontiers left for exploration.

Questions to Be Asked by the Regression Facilitator

As a facilitator of past-life regression, it is your job to direct the subject in such a way that a picture of a lifetime emerges. We do this by asking questions. Although these initial questions sound simple, they may need some explanation.

1. *Where are you?* This question is meant to elicit the immediate environment in which a subject finds himself. For instance, the subject answers, "I am walking along the riverbank." Later, you will have to find out, if possible, the name of the river, the country through which it flows, the city, town, or village in which your regressed subject lives, and so on.

2. *Who are you?* It would be nice to get a name, although the regression may be so primitive that names may not be in use. In some instances, the question will elicit an occupation, such as a soldier, fisherman, or carpenter.

3. *What year is it?* Many answers are straightforward, such as 1797—if the subject belongs to a familiar culture at a relatively recent time. If a past life takes place in China, for example, the answer may confuse you by insisting that it was the "year of the rat." If the memory takes place a few thousand years earlier, the difficulties are seriously compounded. Throughout history, humanity has devised multiple ways of subdividing time, and you won't be able to understand all of them. Worse still, some regression subjects have no interest in dates at all. This may be common among primitive peoples who only followed the seasons because of their importance to agriculture or the movement of game.

   If you get a confusing answer to this question, you're going to have to use your ingenuity to establish a rough date in some other way. One approach is to try to solicit the name of a current ruler, such as a king, queen, or emperor. Another way is to look for recent battles or other large historical events. If all else fails, fashions and clothing or current technology levels often give sufficient clues to narrow down the possibilities. You need to be careful to match technology with a culture. Reference to a main gas supply would strike most of us as modern—part of the Victorian era at the earliest. In fact, gas was available in parts of China as long ago as the fourth century BC. Like much reincarnation research, establishing even a rough date can require patient detective work.

4. *How are you dressed?* This sort of question can often produce important information, but it may also serve only to confuse the picture. Certain styles can be connected to many cultures at many different times. The Greek tunic is a good example. And what do you do with the information that your regressed subject is not dressed at all? This happens during some regressions, and only careful questioning will give you the answer.

5. *What do you look like?* This can frequently result in a vague answer. By no means is this kind of confusion confined to reincarnation research, as an individual's self-image is often very much at variance with reality. It is a good idea to direct the subject's attention to his hands. Be sure to ask about skin color. For example, existing as a black person will not feel any different, and the subject may forget to mention color—which is often a reasonably good indication of a broad geographical location.

6. *What is your occupation?* In some instances, a great deal can be found out from a subject's occupation. One who makes armor, for example, fits into a clearly defined time period, irrespective of culture or geography. Go too far back, and no one wore armor. Come too far forward, and its usage has been abandoned. Once you are able to form a broad picture from the initial contact, you can then experiment by moving a subject backward and forward along the specific lifeline.

7. *What is your age?* If the subject has been regressed to a past life in which he is old and sick, you are unlikely to find out much more about his life by bringing him forward in time. Once you have an age, even an approximate one, you can decide in which direction the key aspects of life will be found. Then it is only a matter of careful questioning before an overall picture of life emerges.

Sooner or later, you will find that you are dealing with a subject who has reached a between-lives state. The person may describe his state as a pleasant pink fog, or he may give a description of leaving the body at the moment of death. There is obviously a vast field of research in this area that needs to be explored.

General Instructions for the Person Being Regressed

Relax. Regression is simply an exercise in exploring your far memory. There are no right or wrong answers. Answer questions about the past with the first impressions that come to mind. Don't try to think out your answers or impressions with generally accepted fact. Information that is at odds with recorded history is often later proved to be accurate. In numerous cases, recorded history has little or nothing to with what actually happened.

You may receive information in any or all of several ways. Some individuals feel that they are actually participating in living a particular lifetime, with all the accompanying sensory input. More commonly, the sensation is one of being an observer and watching the events unfold. Others may have few or no visual impressions but may hear, taste, smell, feel, and sense their surroundings and events. Some will get the main part of their information through physical sensations. Others seem to have no real sensory input but simply "know" the answers to the questions. Of course, many of those who do not receive visual impressions feel disappointed and sometimes allow this disappointment to get in the way of the information they are receiving.

Regression is a way of getting to know yourself. Learn to be sensitive to subtle changes in your senses and your body during the regression experience. These changes are all ways of getting information. Perhaps you are trying to determine where you are in a past life. Maybe you have the sudden sensation of the warmth of the sun on your skin or a light breeze. Chances are that you are outdoors. Perhaps you become aware of a particular smell that is unusual for your physical surroundings.

For instance, if you are in a large city in the here-and-now but you are aware of smelling a barnyard during the regression, it is safe to assume that in the past lifetime you are in or near a barnyard with horses and cattle around. Being sensitive to these subtle impressions. They help you to focus your mind on that particular lifetime. This will in turn encourage more vivid impressions and sensory input. It gets easier with each regression.

What if I can't be regressed? you may ask. We haven't met a person who cannot be regressed, but we have met many people who did not *think* they could be regressed. There have been those who did not believe in reincarnation, those who were opposed to the idea but were willing to try to show that those past-life memories did not exist, and those who did not believe one way or another. Some were convinced that they couldn't be regressed because no one had ever been able to hypnotize them. In our process, we do not hypnotize anyone. We use a multi-awareness program. It is only an exercise in reaching far memory. Every one of the above people has been regressed, and you will be too.

There is very little about the regression experience that is critical. If you become uncomfortable, change positions. If you are itchy, then scratch. If the phone rings, you can relay information through the person who answers it. Just keep your eyes closed, and after the interruption, continue with the regression where you left off.

You are in control during the regression session. You may terminate the session at any time by opening your eyes. If you terminate the session this way, affirm to yourself that you will bring back with you all information that is beneficial to you—and leave behind anything that might be harmful to you in any way. Ending the regression with these statements is often all it takes to free your present self from undesirable feelings, fears, reactions, and attitudes that have their roots in past-life experiences. During the regression, you may refuse to explore any experience that is disagreeable to you or that you choose to explore privately at another time, but don't ignore information you need to think about and deal with.

We do not recommend joint regressions—such as two or more people regressing back to the same lifetime simultaneously, or joint psychic investigations of any type—until the people involved are proficient enough to recognize which impressions are from their own minds and which are from other sources. Often there is telepathy between the two people, working at levels of the mind that can cloud emotions and information. Just as two people looking at a physical object with their physical eyes will have differing perceptions and interpretations, the same is true at the psychic level. By the time a mild emotion toward someone or something has been passed back and forth a time or two, a simple dislike can be distorted into a bitter hatred or a friendship into a grand passion. Each person's mind-voice is as distinctive as his speaking voice, and it is best to experience regressions individually.

Do not use alcohol or drugs before a regression. The effects of these substances on the mind can produce unnecessary complications during the regression, least of which is a distorted experience and unreliable information. At that level of mind, alcohol and drugs diminish your control over the direction of the regression. You could end up triggering some highly traumatic experiences without any mental defenses. Sometimes trivial information can seem to be very important, while critical information can be missed. Experience has shown that often, after the regression, little or no clear perception of the experience is retained.

You should be in control of the regression experience at all times. The person directing you is present as an aid to help you focus your attention, until the time you can regress yourself. If that person attempts to take aggressive control of the regression, persists in asking leading questions, or is not conducting himself properly in some manner, terminate the session and refuse to work with that person in the future.

Be honest with yourself. If you claim impressions that you do not actually experience or make up stories to impress someone, you lose the chance for an exciting and valuable experience. Don't cheat yourself.

Last of all, relax. After a regression or two, you will wonder how you possibly could have been so tense or reluctant to experience something that is so informative and fun.

CHAPTER 14

Death and Rebirth

Most of us fear death and the unknown that comes with it. One of the most rewarding aspects of regression is the ability to explore our death experiences. When the unknowns of death become familiar, we will no longer fear death. Sometimes it may seem that a lot of deaths are violent or traumatic in some way, but this is not the case. Most death experiences we read about in reincarnation research have been chosen to show some traumatic event that managed to influence a present lifetime. These are only a fraction of the total death experiences explored.

The largest number of death experiences are peaceful at the end of the intended life span. This doesn't mean that all planned life spans are long. Life spans are often short because there may be only a limited amount of beneficial experience available within a certain environment for a particular soul. You should not assume that the time of death is set in stone or predestined. Remember, we have free will; it is our rightful heritage. If our time of death was preset, then we would be nothing more than puppets whose strings are controlled by some greater power. All our accomplishments would be meaningless. Life would have no purpose, and we might as well give up now.

What is death? We are unlimited spirits who are manifested in bodies of flesh so we are able to experience the physical world. When our bodies become uninhabitable because of disease, accident, or age, or we just outgrow the usefulness of that body, then we move on to the spirit world and leave our body behind. Death is no more than that. Death and birth are, in fact, synonymous. When we die in the physical world, we are born into the nonphysical world. When we are born into the physical world, we leave the nonphysical world. Death and birth are simply changes in our sphere of activity.

Proof of this is evident in many television shows today, many of which are reality programs that deal with the afterlife. Paranormal investigations have never been more prominent than they are today. Humans have an immortal spirit that survives death.

Exploring Death during the Regression

To explore the death experience during the course of a regression—after the lifetime has been explored—guide the individual through the following verbal directions.

1. Go to the point in time that is one day before your death. It will only take a moment. Tell me as soon as you are there. This is simply an exercise in remembering. There is no reason to feel fear, pain, distress, or apprehension on any level. (Wait for the response)

2. Mentally look out through your eyes and listen through your ears. Where are you, and what are you doing?

3. Approximately what age are you?

4. What is your state of health?

5. Looking back on your life, are there any events not previously remembered that you now remember and would like to mention?

6. How do you feel about your life? Did you accomplish what you intended with this lifetime? (Depending upon the answers, you may want to explore it more fully. Ask any additional questions that seem appropriate at the moment.)

7. Now, without experiencing any pain, distress, fear, or apprehension, pass through the experience of your death and arrive the day after your death. It will only take a moment. Tell me when you are there. This is simply an exercise in remembering.

8. Are you aware that you are dead?

9. How did you die?

10. How do you feel about being dead?

Most people, but not all, are aware that they are dead. They don't seem to be surprised that their consciousness has continued. Occasionally, when death has happened suddenly through accident or violence, the individual may not be aware of the change. The change in consciousness between life and death is so minimal that the only difference is a sense of freedom, of no longer being limited by the physical body. The person may even attempt to carry out physical actions or communicate with individuals in the vicinity and be frustrated and confused by the lack of response. If this situation has occurred in the death experience being investigated, instruct the subject to move to the point in time when he became aware that he was dead. Ask what caused him to become aware that he was dead.

When the subject is immediately aware of his deaths, which occurs in the majority of cases, we find that the person's consciousness often remains to observe the actions of friends and relatives. It is not unusual at all for an individual to observe his own funeral. It is common for people being regressed not to show any distress during the death experience—or afterward at the idea of being dead. As strange as it may seem, the period immediately after death provides some very funny moments through the observations and comments of the deceased. After the individual has passed through the death experience, say to him: "Go to go to a point in time about six weeks after your death. It will only take a moment. Tell me as soon as you are there. Where are you, and what are you doing?

At this point there will probably be very little sensory input. People usually describe a feeling of just "being." There are no sensations of heat or cold or sound, and there are usually no visual sensations. This seems to be a period of rest from the earthly experience. Occasionally there may be a vague awareness of others in a similar state nearby. However, even when there is no consciousness or other awareness, subjects do not express feelings of loneliness or of being alone. From this point on, time spans are meaningless, for time as we know it does not exist. Time is a concept created for the physical man.

At some point, the person will emerge from the rest period to undertake an evaluation of the preceding lifetime and to look at the bigger picture of other lifetimes. This is the time for self-judgment in which the person truly meets himself and relives the pros and cons of the previous life. This is often a profound experience, since there are no illusions. The person reliving the episode may not want to talk about the details, but it is important for them to record it privately for future study. This may not be an unpleasant experience. As people review their decisions, they may be surprised to find that everything comes out on the positive side. To direct an individual to this experience, say: "Now move to the period in which you begin your evaluation of your past lifetime."

Exploring Birth during the Regression

The steps of a person's blueprint for life may not manifest in a particular order, but after self-evaluation, an individual will often find himself in some type of learning experience. This may be in a group format or an individual class set up for students to live through and understand a truth or concept.

Sometime before or after this period, the blueprint for the next lifetime will have begun. The general circumstances for the next lifetime are chosen: race, social status, economic conditions, probable career, type of parents, and so forth. It isn't necessary to explore this aspect at this point. The time for that is later, when the blueprint is complete.

Since man has free will, in or out of the physical body, unwise choices may be made when developing the blueprint. Only in rare, extreme circumstances does there seem to be any type of guidance from outside sources. Often remorse or a great deal of excitement will cause a soul to undertake situations based on unrealistic expectations of what they can complete. People can choose difficult circumstances for a lifetime and overload themselves with what they want to accomplish in one lifetime. They end up overwhelmed, discouraged, and frustrated, and they accomplish very little. On the other extreme, some may choose life circumstances that provide ease with little challenge. This type of life can be unfulfilling.

A soul is not locked into a blueprint, even after birth. Unwise choices can be changed, and life directions can be altered. Knowledge can bring understanding, which can change a person's outlook. For example, a person can recognize that he is continually involved in cycles of unhappiness or suffering, having unwisely chosen that method of Karmic penance for past actions. Realizing that Karma is intended to teach rather than punish, and that a positive approach is more desirable, a person can mentally reject another cycle of the same and choose a positive course of action. When a person recognizes the beginning of a cycle that deals with lessons already learned, he can mentally say, *I do not choose to participate in this cycle. It has no positive benefit for me. I choose to move forward with something else.* This is enough to change the sequence of events.

Since individuals are different in how they deal with a wide variety of experiences, it is very difficult for a facilitator to customize the process for a specific person. Toward the end of a regression, after exploring the death experience, direct the subject (or yourself) with the following verbal instructions.

1. Come forward now to the point in time when you chose your parents for this present lifetime as_____ (the subject's present name). It will only take a moment. Tell me as soon as you are there.

2. At that time, why did you choose these people to be your parents? (The answers will be all over the place. The choice may have been made before the parents even met each other, or the choice may not have been made until the pregnancy was established. It varies from person to person. Sometimes information obtained is known only to the subject's parents, and it can be verified by them if they are open to sharing this type of information—private conversations, private jokes, a favorite dress or tie, the circumstances of their first meeting, and so on.)

3. What lessons did you hope to learn from the particular environment these parents could provide? (The subject may or may not choose to answer these questions aloud.)

4. At this time, you have access to the blueprint you created for this particular lifetime. Examine it until you have firmly fixed your awareness on what you wanted to accomplish in this lifetime. You may verbalize the information or not, but tell me when you have the information set in your mind.

5. You may return to this point of awareness any time you desire additional information.

Now, go ahead and terminate the session in the same manner outlined in the standard regression technique, offering the following verbal advice:

"This information can be a valuable insight into your life. You may find that you have already accomplished most of what you intended and are free to set new goals. Maybe you will find some underlying problems in your life. Maybe you changed direction from your blueprint, and the things you wanted to accomplish are causing undefined thoughts in your mind, which may keep you from feeling satisfied with your direction. Has the deviation taken you in a positive direction? Was the deviation by your own will or was it the result of actions by others. You may find that others made choices and changes between the time you chose your parents and the time you were born. These changes may have been so radically different that you had to create a whole new plan.

"If the direction or your life is good, despite the deviation, or if it is a matter beyond your control, then mentally affirm that you are letting go of the original blueprint and following a course of action that is more appropriate for now. This mental letting-go will get rid of many, if not all, of those semi-subconscious frustrations that make you feel that you are not doing what you ought to be doing with your life.

"But if you find that you have deviated from your blueprint for no good reason, and you are not making progress in your spiritual growth, then you have to take a look at your blueprint and your life and do whatever you need to do to bring them closer together. There may be compromises you have to make. You will see that it's not a matter of what you do but how you do it. Your attitude toward life will make the difference in how much harmony you have with your blueprint. Be fair, tolerant, and kind. Always want the best for yourself and others. Always think in a positive way, and imagine yourself as successful. Everything is created in the mind first. Hold the thought of yourself being successful, no matter what you do. The changes will not happen immediately, but over time you will see the changes you imagined.

The Length of Time between Lifetimes

There seems to be no standard length of time between lifetimes. Sometimes centuries pass between lifetimes, and at other times, only a few months go by. A soul may have to wait for just the right set of circumstances to occur, or perhaps a certain world event. If the person died prematurely, leaving things undone that were very important to them, then the time between lifetimes may be short. If a prior lifetime was difficult or unpleasant or left a traumatic scar on the soul, then the soul may be reluctant to reincarnate. This may account for some stillbirths or newborn deaths that occur for no physical reason. The soul panics and backs out.

In war, where death occurs in the defense of the country or an ideal that is important to the person, the soul may return quickly to continue the situation. Others may return quickly in an effort to stop such conflicts. Some of the protesters of the 1960s, when regressed, were found to be casualties of World War II and the Korean conflict. The exploration of death and what happens afterward can be as exciting as the investigations of past lives themselves.

Your Soul Origin

It is possible to know your soul's blueprint and everything you need to know about your soul's destiny. Regression will provide an opportunity to align your soul with your past lives. I like the way Levi H. Dowling describes the soul as "that from which all things are formed … It is the first stage of the crystallization of spirit … It is exquisite fineness that is so sensitive that the slightest vibrations any place in the universe register an impression upon it. It is energy in its first and earliest state, before our individual thoughts and emotions affect our future lives. This energy has aliveness, vitality, individualized uniquely as specific souls."

This is where we become aware that we exist as individual souls. After we have experienced a number of regressions and feel very comfortable with the process, we can return to the point of our soul's origin instead of emerging in a past lifetime. When we arrive at that point, we can hear the instructions given to us. It seems that we souls were sent out on a field trip to explore, discover, and understand all of creation. Some of us have completed our assignments and have returned to the source. Others of us have lost our way, not knowing why we are here, what we are, or where we come from, and so we remain here, trying to find our way back.

As unlimited spirits, many of us are intrigued by the physical creatures we observe. At some point, our creator created human bodies as vehicles for our souls, giving us the opportunity for a much larger experience in the earth plane. Yet we all, at one time or another, feel a profound loneliness, seldom understanding what it is. That intense loneliness that we can't describe is our feeling of separation from our creator. Our souls wish to return to our creator.

We experience this longing to varying degrees throughout our many lifetimes. How much we feel this loneliness is based on how far away we get from our creator. The actions we take in the physical world reflect the distance we are from our creator. There are those who seek extreme success to fill that vacancy. Others go from person to person, trying to find someone who can fill the hole. Lives are filled with people, noise, alcohol, drugs, and activities in attempts to fill the emptiness. The more that people pursue these actions to fill the emptiness, the further they move away and create barriers to their creator. Remember that when your mind is full of "stuff," you will never learn how to be at peace with yourself. Your mind has to be quiet, enabling you to find and contact your real self.

Past-life regression not only has the ability to allow a person to recall the experiences of past lifetimes, but it opens access to those deeper levels of the mind where we can communicate with our spiritual selves. This is where the awareness of being part of something whole brings a deep sense of contentment and fulfillment. You will find that you stop wanting all the toys, the big house, and expensive vacations. You know that you no longer need to bury yourself in material objects to find fulfillment.

CHAPTER 15

Dreams and Regression

When James S. was twenty years old, he awoke one morning to recall part of a vivid dream. He dreamed that he was an old man in a military uniform, walking down a hill and hiding behind trees. He felt weak, but he did not know who he was or what he was doing there. His recall of the dream ended there.

James was interested in the dream because it was so real. But couldn't understand it, so he soon forgot it. Over the years, James found himself having the same dream over and over again. As time when on, the dream unfolded, and James eventually reached the bottom of the hill. He had a hard time walking, and he knew he had to reach the other side of the field, although he did not know why. Halfway across the field, James collapsed on the grass, lay there for a moment, and died. After James's dream-death, he found himself floating above and looking down on his dead body in the grass. He still did not know who he was or what he was doing there, but oddly, all sense of urgency had vanished. Whatever he had been trying to do didn't matter anymore.

The Dream Breakthrough

Even though James had watched his own death, he didn't find the dream disturbing, but he *was* intrigued by the fact that the dream had continued for so many years. James subsequently became the subject in a series of regressions. They showed that the dream was James's first spontaneous recall of far memory. We do not know why this happened. Many people go through life without even wondering if they have lived before, let alone remembering any of the details. My thought is that there comes a time in our spiritual development where we start to integrate past-life memories. There may come a time when, in order for us to expand our viewpoint, we must open up to our past memories.

The reason for spontaneous recall of far memory may be more psychological. It may start with neuroses that send signals to the conscious mind. These signals can easily be from a former life, as was James's experience. Whatever the reason, past-life signals do occur more often than we realize. James is only one in a large number of documented cases. Nowhere is this breakthrough in recall more likely to happen than in a dream. It's like your mind is trying to tell you that you have lived before by showing you a little piece of what your past life looked like. Such dreams are distinctive and may be used as a valid tool in the investigation of your past lives.

Distinguishing a Reincarnation Dream from Other Dreams

There are many factors that determine the recall of a dream as a reincarnation dream. The first thing to look for is a realistic tone to the dream. This dream may be vivid and may feel intensely real. We tend to remember it far longer than the average dream. The details are clear and remain clear. James's dream was extremely vivid. When he awoke, he remembered every detail.

The next thing to look for is lucidity. An almost overriding characteristic of dreams is their built-in element of unreality. This is not usually apparent while we are actually dreaming. Something about the dream state allows us to accept the most bizarre things that happen in the dream. But later, when we wake, it is easy to see that the dream had a melting, shifting quality. One minute we are in Toronto, and the next minute we are in New York—without knowing how we got there.

Other than when James looked down on his body, there were no unbelievable parts to the dream. Time flowed as it should. Things in the dream remained as they were, without changing into something else. With the exception of those final moments, he might have been experiencing reality—and I will have something to say about those final moments later.

Ending Recurring Dreams

Reincarnation dreams occur out of signals in the depths of our psyche. The dreams try to draw the attention of the conscious mind. Maybe the dream is trying to say that the time has come for us to begin thinking a little further than the here-and-now, but very few of us pay attention. Or if we do, very few of us understand at once what the dream was all about. So it continues to repeat itself until the message gets through. Although James endured this repeating dream for most of his life, it finally stopped with his first experience of conscious regression, and it has not recurred since. James's personal awareness of the reincarnation process relieved the pressure of the signals.

What to Look For

A vivid, lucid, or recurring dream, by itself, means little. But when you find all three together, you may begin to suspect far memory. An important factor is how you see yourself in the dream.

Do you see yourself seated in a theater, watching a movie or a play? One of the characters is playing you on stage, but the real you is somewhere outside, an observer. The situation is very distinctive and represents another characteristic of far memory. Seeing yourself in a dream as an actor or actress, do you look as you look now? Do you have the same build, hair, and so on? When you analyze your dream for far memory, you are not looking for differences in the way you perceive yourself. You are looking for a wholly different person. I find it interesting that the man in James's dream never grew any older as James grew older. It was like watching a movie over and over again.

Another important consideration is the way your dream-self acts—perhaps even opposite to who you really are. Your dream-self may have picked up habits that are not apparent in your waking life. In the dream, your usual interests may have changed. Subtle changes of this type are always worth exploring, if you are looking for far memory. But the dominant characteristics of your dream-self and real self are often the same. In James's dream, he was determined to climb down the hill and cross to the other side of the field—and died trying. This same determination is very obvious in the waking James.

Differences arise in culturally conditioned behavior. An example might be the hat-sweeping bow that was the custom of French noblemen in the seventeenth century. This custom seems over-the-top for us now, so its appearance in a dream might well be taken as uncharacteristic behavior. With so much emphasis placed on differences, we might do well to note that, no matter how different the central character of a reincarnation dream may look or behave, we will have no doubts about the character's identity. There is something in each of us that reaches down through the years and triggers instant recognition of what we once were.

Dream Details

So far, we have looked at the larger picture of the reincarnation dream. Now it's time to look at specifics. Let's start with how a person is dressed in the dream. What we are looking for is a style of dress that indicates a different time in history. Check your footwear and all details of your clothing.

Let's review. Reincarnation dreams are vivid, lucid, and recurring. You should pay attention to how you see yourself, how you look, how you behave, what you are wearing, the environment (place and time) of the dream, the content of the dream, and the central character's main concern.

Dreams are important, and a great deal of research has gone into them. However, no one is sure how they play in the human psyche. We do know that dreams carry (often symbolic) messages from one level of our mind to another. Some dreams reflect our waking interests and concerns.

The first challenge is to catch the dream. Of course, this is easy if it's a spectacular, recurring dream. Such dreams force themselves on your consciousness, and continue to do so—often over many years—until you start to take them seriously. But the odds are that you will have very few such dreams. Therefore, you will have to look through more routine dreams. You are going to have to learn one more technique, one that will let you catch your dream. This technique for remembering is simple to describe, but it takes a lot of determination to follow through. If you do follow it through, it will open up a whole area of interest and experience that has been lost to you for years.

When you go to bed tonight—and every night hereafter—keep a special notebook and pen or pencil beside your bed. Have it close enough so you don't have to get out of bed to reach it. When you awake in the middle of the night or in the morning, make a note of any dream memories you may have. The trick is to do it at once. If you wait even thirty seconds, the dream could be lost.

This sounds easy enough, but when you're relaxed and sleepy, it will be difficult to do. Learn to write in the dark. Develop the ability to make points that will jog your memory. The more you do it, the easier it will become. After a while, it will just become habit, and you will wonder why you thought it was so difficult.

Now, having captured your dreams, write them up in detail in your regression book. When you have written them up, use some of the ideas we have discussed to sift out any elements that seem to suggest far memory. Make a note alongside the dream itself. It is a rare thing for dream analysis to present you positive proof of a past life, but as you become more skilled, you will be surprised to discover how many interesting pointers you will find. What you are doing is creating a comprehensive record of your inner life.

CHAPTER 16

Your First Regression

You have finally made it. You are now ready for your first direct experience of a past life. Find a friend and a willing subject. Then, use the multi-level awareness exercises in this chapter as a guide—and begin.

Multi-Level Regression Technique

This technique has been used by Florence McClain, a noted writer.

Have your subject assume a comfortable position and verbally guide him through this relaxation exercise.

1. Close your eyes. Direct your awareness to your eyelids. (Pause for 2–3 seconds.) Notice any muscles that may be tense. Pause to relax your eyelids. Relax each muscle so that your eyelids become completely relaxed. (Pause.)

2. Direct your awareness to your scalp. (Pause.) Notice any muscles that may be tense. Especially notice the small muscles

around the edge of the scalp. (Pause.) Relax your scalp. Relax each muscle so that your scalp becomes completely relaxed. (Pause.)

3. Direct your awareness to your face. (Pause.) Notice any muscles that may be tense. (Pause.) Allow the muscles of your face to become completely relaxed. (Pause.)

4. Direct your awareness to your neck. Become aware of the muscles that control your neck. (Pause.) Relax your neck. Relax each muscle. Allow your neck to become completely relaxed. (Pause.)

5. Direct your awareness to your hands. (Pause.) Become aware of the many small muscles and bones in your hands. (Pause.) Relax your hands. Allow your hands to become completely relaxed. (Pause.)

6. Direct your awareness to your chest, an area containing muscles, organs, glands, and nerves. (Pause.) Relax each muscle, each organ, each gland, and each nerve. Allow your chest to become completely relaxed. (Pause.)

7. Direct your awareness to your abdomen, an area containing muscles, organs, glands, and nerves. (Pause.) Relax each muscle, each organ, each gland, and each nerve. Allow your abdomen to completely relax. (Pause.)

8. Direct your awareness to your legs. (Pause.) Notice any muscles that may be tense. (Pause.) Relax your legs. Allow your legs to become completely relaxed. (Pause.)

9. Direct your attention to your feet, an area of small muscles and bones. (Pause.) Notice any muscles that may be tense. (Pause.) Relax your feet. Allow your feet to be completely relaxed. (Pause.)

10. It is a wonderful feeling to be relaxed, a very natural and healthy state of being. Anytime you desire to return to this

state of relaxation, all you have to do is take a deep breath, and as you exhale, mentally repeat the word *relax* three times, and you will become completely relaxed

11. You are in complete control at every level of your mind. You are relaxed but mentally alert and aware. Should you choose to terminate this session, you need only to open your eyes. Should someone call you in case of danger or an emergency, you will immediately be alert and aware and fully oriented to the present time and place.

12. I may terminate this session by counting aloud from one to five or by touching one of your shoulders three times. At the count of five—or when you feel my hand touch your shoulder for the third time—your eyes will open, and you will be alert and refreshed.

13. You will bring with you from the regression experience everything that will be beneficial to you in any way. You will leave behind everything that might be detrimental to you in any way.

Insist that your subject respond to you verbally as he completes each step of the exercise. Don't allow yourself to be bogged down in this exercise. If the individual indicates some difficulty, just tell him to pretend or imagine that his feet are no longer part of his body (see the second step below). When there is a verbal response, continue with the regression. You will start this part with the following verbal directions.

1. At this time I am going to direct you through some mental exercises. Tell me when you have completed each exercise. They will only take a moment.

2. Become unaware of your feet. Cause your feet to feel as though they do not belong to your body. It will only take a moment. Tell me when you have done this.

3. Good. Your feet now feel as if they do not belong to your body.

4. Become unaware of your legs. Cause your legs to feel as though they do not belong to your body. It will only take a moment. Tell me when you have done this. (Pause to wait for a response.) Good. Your feet and legs now feel as though they do not belong to your body.

5. Become unaware of your abdomen. Cause your abdomen to feel as though it does not belong to your body. It will only take a moment. Tell me when you have done this. (Pause for a response.) Good. Your feet, legs, and abdomen feel as though they do not belong to your body.

6. Become unaware of your chest. Cause your chest to feel as though it does not belong to your body. Tell me when you have done this. It will only take a moment. (Pause for a response.) Good. Your feet, legs, abdomen, and chest now feel as if they do not belong to your body. It's a wonderful feeling to be relaxed—a very natural, healthy state of being.

7. Now quickly imagine that you are standing in front of the building where you presently live. It will only take a moment. Tell me as soon as you are there. (Pause for a response.) Good. Now, briefly describe the front door of the building to me. Tell me what you would see if you were physically standing in front of the building where you live now. (Pause for a brief description.) What season of the year is it? (At this point, begin with the season of the year named, and substitute it in the proper sequence in the rest of the exercise.)

8. It's fall? Fine. Now imagine it is winter. It will only take a moment. Describe how the appearance of the building and surrounding area differs in the winter. (Pause for a brief response.)

9. Good. Now imagine that it is spring. Describe how the appearance differs in the spring. (Pause for a brief response.)

10. Good. Now imagine that it is summer. Describe how the appearance differs in the summer. (Pause for a brief response.)

11. Now, imagine that it is fall again.

When these preliminary exercises have been completed at the first regression, it is not necessary to repeat them for subsequent regressions. Simply tell the person to relax by taking a deep breath and then exhaling while mentally repeating the word *relax* three times. At this point, if the regression is to be recorded, turn on the recorder.

1. Imagine that you are standing in front of the door of your home. Imagine that you are opening the door. Imagine that the door opens into a long tunnel, and you see a light at the end of the tunnel. I am going to count from twenty down to one. With each descending number, imagine that you are moving down the tunnel toward the light, moving back in time to a lifetime you lived previous to this one. At the count of one, you will step from the tunnel into the light, into a lifetime that you lived previous to this one.

2. Twenty (pause), nineteen (pause), eighteen. You are moving toward the light, back through time to a lifetime you lived previous to this one. Seventeen (pause), sixteen (pause), fifteen. You are moving toward the light and back through time. Fourteen (pause), thirteen (pause), twelve. At the count of one, you will be in a lifetime you lived previous to this one. Eight (pause), seven (pause), six, back through time, five (pause), four (pause), three. At the count of one, you will step from the tunnel into the light, into a lifetime that you lived previous to this one. Two (pause), one. You are now in a lifetime that you lived previous to this one.

3. Mentally look out through your eyes and listen through your ears. Mentally look down at your feet. What are you wearing on your feet? (Pause for a response, and then continue with the following questions.)

- What are you wearing on your body?
- About what age are you?
- Are you male or female?
- What is your name—the first name that comes to mind? Mentally look out through your eyes and listen through your ears.
- Where are you? Describe your surroundings.
- What part of the world are you in?
- Do you know what year or time period it is?
- What does your mother look like?
- How do you feel about her?
- What does your father look like?
- How do you feel about him?
- Do you have any brothers or sisters?
- Do you have any close friends?

Any one of these questions, when answered, may lead you in any direction. Follow the subject in the direction he is going.

Once I asked a client what he was wearing, and he started to describe elaborate armor. He was at war with England, fighting for a free Scotland, and I spent a couple of hours listening to a detailed description of the time. We never got past the first question. So be open and intuitive on where to take the regression.

Continue the regression with these verbal directions and questions.

1. Now quickly scan one day in your life. It will only take a moment. How do you spend your time?

2. Move forward in time to the point where you are approximately five years older, about the age of [fill in the blank]. It will only take a moment. You will feel time passing around you like

currents of air or the pages flipping off a calendar. Tell me as soon as you are there.

3. Mentally look out through your eyes and listen through your ears.

   - Where are you, and what are you doing?

   - Are you married?

   - Do you have children?

   - Do you believe in a higher power?

   - Do you belong to a formal religion?

   - Are you happy?

4. Quickly scan the next ten, fifteen, or twenty years (whatever is appropriate to the person's age in the regression). It will only take a moment. Tell me about any outstanding events or accomplishments that you would like to share. Is there anything you want to do that you haven't been able to do? Is there anything you have done that makes you feel proud?

Remember that these are only sample questions to be used as a guide. These questions are intended to elicit general information and will lead to certain lines of questioning. At this time, direct the person into another past lifetime. Continue with the same type of questioning by saying: "At this time, go back in time to a lifetime you lived previous to this one. It will only take a moment. Tell me as soon as you are there. You will arrive at age twelve."

When you are ready to terminate the regression say: "In a moment I will count from one to five. At the count of five, you will open your eyes in the here-and-now, feeling alert and refreshed. You will bring with you everything on every level that is beneficial to you in any way. You will leave behind everything that is detrimental to you in any way. One, two, three. At the count of five, you will be in your present lifetime as [insert person's name], feeling refreshed and alert. Four, five. Eyes open, feeling refreshed and alert.

Immediately following the regression is a good time to make a note of any additional information that the person may have remembered but didn't mention during the regression. Also note anyone the subject recognized during the regression as being someone known in this present lifetime.

A person may feel uncomfortable or embarrassed after the regression, as if he made the whole thing up. This is common, but the feeling fades as spontaneous memories begin to occur.

The first regression is basically intended to elicit general information to be used later for more detailed regressions. You may revisit any lifetime by saying, "You will be in the lifetime you lived as [insert name]. If no name was remembered, you may identify the lifetime by a time period, location, or any identifying feature.

The subject may have an attraction to a certain time period or location, and you may direct the person there by saying, "You will be in a lifetime during [insert time period] or in [insert place]. Always use the phrase "may have lived." The attraction may be there for other reasons than a past life. You do not want to confuse the subconscious by telling it to remember a lifetime that never existed.

A good technique is to direct the person back to a lifetime that is most important to him today in his lifetime as [insert current name].

If the person being regressed has a specific problem he wants to investigate, direct him to go to the point in time where the problem started. This should not be done until the person has had some regression experiences and feels comfortable. If the problem is traumatic in this current lifetime, then the odds are it will be even more traumatic at the point of origin. Be sure to remind the person that this experience is an exercise in remembering. There is no need to feel any stress of any kind. He is physically in the here-and-now and should look at the situation as if he is watching a movie.

If, during the regression, you direct the person to move ahead a few years in that lifetime and he arrives at a blank spot with no sensory input, it is probably after the death experience. Just direct the person to move back to another lifetime.

During the first regression it is not unusual for there to be no response to certain questions. If no response is elicited to one or more questions, just say, "That's all right," and move on. As with any new experience, it may take a time or two to become good at recalling information. The better you get at remembering, the more detailed the information becomes. Some people remember exact birthdates, times, and places.

CHAPTER 17

True Stories of Past Lives

This is the fun part: when you regress someone and you are able to verify the information, proving that they have lived before.

Here are some cases you will find interesting. They have been independently investigated for well-documented proof that the individuals lived previous lives. There are thousands of cases just like the ones you are about to read about, cases that prove that we have these memories of past times, people, and places.

These cases reflect experiences similar to what I have found in some of my own regressions, which I will cover a little later in the book.

I find that the most fascinating stories come from children who remember being here before. Children have always had great imaginations, and they don't have any agenda in telling their stories.

James Leininger

Here's a true story of an eight-year-old boy who remembers his life as a fighter pilot. James Leininger lives in Louisiana, and for the past five years, he has been talking about his dreams and memories of being a man called Lieutenant James McCready Huston, a World War II fighter pilot from Uniontown who was killed in Iwo Jima. At only two and half years old, the boy began talking about aviation, and his knowledge of the subject was amazing. He had never been taught this, as his parents knew nothing about aviation.

He started to have nightmares about being shot down by a Japanese plane with a red sun on it. James's father started to look into what his son was talking about and was floored when he finally realized that something unbelievable was happening. There was no way James could have known these historic facts. His nightmares started after his father had taken him to the Dallas flight museum, but there wasn't any information there that could have started these vivid memories.

His mother, Andrea, recalled how James would scream at the top of his voice, "Airplane crash! On fire. Can't get out. Help!" One time when his mother took him shopping, she pointed at a plane in a store window. "Look," she said, "the plane has a bomb at the bottom." She was shocked to hear her two-and-a-half-year-old son say, "That's not a bomb. That's a drop tank." Andrea had no idea what a drop tank was, and James later went on to tell his parents that he had flown a plane called a Corsair that took off from a boat called Natoma. When his parents made meat loaf for dinner, a dish he had never had before, James said, "Meatloaf. I haven't had that since I was on Natoma."

Bruce, James's father, decided to do some research of his own. He found out that there had been a small escort carrier called Natoma Bay, which had been in the battle of Iwo Jima. Further research divulged that there had indeed been a pilot called James Huston. His plane had been hit in the engine by Japanese fire on March 3, 1945.

In a further twist to the story, Huston's sister, Anne Barron, who is now eighty-seven years old, was found, and she stated that after listening to little James's story, she totally believes him. He knows too many things, and for some reason he has all the details of what happened. Huston's cousin Bob, now seventy-four years old, also had this to say: "To me, it's amazing. Everything the boy said is exactly the account told to James Huston's father and also to my mother. There is no way the child could have that information."

When James was six years old in 2004, his father took him to a reunion of veterans who served on the Natoma. When he was there, James was able to recognize one of his old mates after sixty years. James said to his parents, "They have gotten so old."

James's father, Bruce Leininger, is said to be writing a book about the experience.

Cameron Macaulay

This is another story of a child's past-life memories. Cameron lived his whole life in Glasgow, Scotland, but at the age of two, he told his family about his previous life on the Island of Barra, which is situated on the west coast of Scotland. Cameron started talking about a white house that overlooked the sea and the beach. He said that airplanes used to land on the beach and that he loved his black-and-white dog. The family had never been to Barra, which was two hundred miles away from their home.

Cameron's father on the Island of Barra was named Shane Robertson, and he had died by being hit by a car. Cameron kept complaining that on Barra they'd had three toilets. Cameron drew the house that he had lived in. It was a long, white house right on the beach. He would talk about his parents and brothers and sisters. Cameron was upset and cried continuously for his mother, who had read Bible stories to him. But his mother in the present never read the Bible to him.

Finally, Cameron was taken to the Island of Barra. When they arrived at the house, Cameron jumped out of the car and ran straight into the house. He recognized it immediately. But as Cameron walked through the door, he began to grow pale and quiet. I guess Cameron realized that his past-life family no longer lived there. Then he took off running around the house, pointing out all the rooms where he had lived—all the nooks and crannies and the three toilets. Much to his mother's surprise, when he went into the garden, he took them to a secret entrance that he had been talking about for years.

The last thing Cameron had mentioned to a friend was, "Don't worry about dying. You just come back again." When his mother asked him how he'd gotten here, he said, "I just fell through into your tummy."

Jenny Cockell

Jenny Cockell was an ordinary homemaker and mother of two living in Northamptonshire. Over the course of several years, she came to believe that she had lived before as an Irish woman named Mary Sutton who had been born in 1897—and found that she still had children living in Ireland.

Her story starts with her fourth birthday, when she began to remember her past life. For a long time, she didn't tell anyone, because she believed that everybody had the same feelings and experiences.

The most vivid of the memories was a disturbing one. She dreamed of her death—or, should I say, Mary's death. She was also aware that Mary was thirty-five years old and had just given birth to her eighth child. She could see the hospital where it was all happening. Mary had strong feelings of deep sorrow that she was leaving her children without a mother.

Those feelings never left Jenny, and much later she decided to draw a map where she believed all of this had happened. She only knew that it had been in Ireland and that she had felt bad for leaving her children. Jenny realized then that she had to go back to Ireland, so she got a map of Ireland and pointed out a town called Malahide, which she just knew was her hometown. But Jenny was still a child.

A number of years later, after Jenny got married and had her own children, the feeling and memories surfaced more clearly than ever. So Jenny started to think about tracking down Mary's family in Ireland. Jenny said that if she were to trace the family, she wanted to make sure she did it right—no mistakes and not the smallest doubt. It had to be the right house and the right family, with all the correct names, dates, and children's names. So Jenny consulted with a past life regression facilitator who would regress her back.

At the time, Jenny was very much a skeptic. She really didn't believe that anything like reincarnation or other types of psychic phenomena existed. That's what makes this story so incredible. Jenny felt uncomfortable with the whole story and was afraid she would make a fool of herself.

After undergoing regression, Jenny realized that these memories were not going away. She decided to go to Ireland. She looked at the maps she had drawn from past memory and compared them with a real map of the town of Malahide. She was amazed to find that the maps were almost identical. This was what she needed to finally commit to going to Ireland—a journey back in time to see if she could find the home and family she had left many years before.

Jenny arrived in Malahide, which is north of Dublin, and decided to check the church records. The records showed that a Mary Sutton had lived and died in Malahide. Her eight children had been left to various relatives, and some had been placed in orphanages. Jenny wanted to try to find her children and other relatives, so she decided to go to the newspapers and television stations. She wrote to all the churches in the area.

Jenny was shocked when she located the surviving children. Before she met the children, she was questioned by the British Broadcasting Network to make sure that the dreams and memories she'd been having matched up with the facts from the surviving members of the Irish family.

Jenny told the researchers facts about the family home, the kind of sewing thread that Mary had used, and even small events—like when the children had caught a live rabbit in a trap.

Eventually, after her interview, Jenny came face-to-face with Sonny, Mary's son, for the first time.

In 1990 Sonny Sutton picked up the phone and listened to the most amazing story he had ever heard. When he finally hung up the phone, his wife said to him, "It looks like you have seen a ghost." White as a sheet, Sonny turned to his wife and said, "I have been just talking to my mother."

The rest of Mary's family were not so easily convinced. They wanted to know who Jenny was and the reason she was doing this to their family. They just could not believe that this could be possible. The family had been raised Catholic, and in complete shock, Mary's daughter Phyllis Clinton went to see her priest. After reviewing the evidence, he told her that somehow Mary was speaking through Jenny as a way of uniting the family.

Christy (72), Frank (70), Phyllis (71), Betty Keogh (62), and their brother Jeffery James (who died in 1992 at age 66) were very unsettled by the whole thing. Jenny knew the pictures that were on the walls, what was in the house, and how it was built. "It is unbelievable," said Phyllis. "Even though I know it is the truth, I still find it very difficult to believe. It looks like my mother Mary passed her soul over to an unborn child who was Jenny."

There was a twenty-one-year gap between the time when Mary died and Jenny was born. This story is very unusual, in that the children could be found to corroborate the story.

Jenny is a member of Mensa. She is very down-to-earth, and she made sure that anything she could not remember was not to be added to the story—only things that were proven beyond a shadow of doubt.

This is truly a fascinating story. Born into a normal household, an average woman grew up with the idea that it was normal to remember past lives. What's even more important is that after Mary's death, her children were separated and lost contact with each other for nearly sixty years. Jenny Cockell did a remarkable thing: she reunited a lost family. The family vowed never to be apart again.

Kim's Story

This regression was from one of my clients. Of course, the names and country of origin have been changed to protect his privacy. You must ensure that your clients have the same protection of privacy as lawyers and doctors provide to their patients.

I will give you a little background information on this case. The person involved had emigrated from another country. His wife said he wanted to come to the United States because he had an overwhelming interest in the American Civil War. Every time they had any time off, all he wanted to do was find Civil War memorabilia. To say that the man was obsessed with the Civil War would be putting it mildly. The wife said that when they went to many of these war sites, her husband just stood there with a faraway look in his eyes. It seemed to her that his depression became more pronounced after a visit to a Civil War battleground.

The man's wife, whom we will call Li, said that her husband, whom we will call Kim, was initially very excited to get to those locations but that he was now always depressed. He didn't even want to get out of bed in the morning. They had gone to different doctors, and all of them recommended antidepressants. Li said that her husband had been on them for over six months, with no improvement. She didn't know what to do.

Li happened to be working with someone who knew about past-life regression, who understood that the problems we have in this lifetime might not be from this lifetime at all. Li's coworker knew me and suggested she call me for a chat. Of course, Li thought her coworker was a little crazy, but by that time, she had nothing to lose.

Li called me and set an appointment for her husband. When Kim arrived, he looked like the weight of the world was on his shoulders. We talked a little bit about his situation, as I wanted to make sure he felt totally comfortable with me and the regression. I always remind people that it is nothing more than an exercise in far memory.

I took Kim through the relaxing techniques found in this book. The first regression with someone new always takes a little more time, because we have to take them through the whole process. Once we have completed it once, we can go back and start up anytime.

What follows is the record of Kim's regression.

Me: Three, two, one. You are now in a lifetime you lived previous to this one. Mentally look out through your eyes and mentally listen with your ears. Mentally look down at your feet. What are you wearing on your feet?

Kim: It looks like boots, but right now I am hiding.

Me: From whom?

Kim: The Billys.

Me: Who are the Billys?

Kim: The Billy Yanks, the union soldiers.

Me: Why are you hiding?

Kim: They're coming to destroy our town of Marianna.

Me: Where is Marianna?

Kim: In Florida.

Me: Do you know what year it is?

Kim: It's 1864, and we are waiting for them to come down our street so we can attack them. We have to stop them. The Yanks kill and destroy everything. They care nothing for life.

Me: Why are you fighting?

Kim: Their president wants to tax everything we do and ship. It's causing everyone to feel lost, with no control over what happens in our lives. We can't allow this to happen. We will have no food or the ability to buy anything. Our cotton will rot in the fields. I have to be quiet. They're coming.

Me: Remember, Kim. Just think of it as watching a movie. Nothing can hurt you. You are with me in the here-and-now. Anytime you want to end the regression, just open your eyes.

Kim: I hear gunfire. They are getting close. I am so scared. The Yanks are killers.

Me: Is there anyone with you?

Kim: Yes. There's a fifteen-year-old boy here. He's been with me, and I am trying to protect him the best I can. Sully, look out! They are coming up behind you.

Me: What's happening now?

Kim: The Billys are charging down our main street, and they are sneaking up behind us. Fire, Sully. Reload. Shoot, Sully. Run and follow me. My God, everyone is running and yelling. There's nonstop gunfire. The Billys are burning down all the buildings. Sully, come with me into the church. Take a window, and keep shooting. Don't let them get close to us. It looks like the colored troops have finally made our boys give up. We aren't going to give up.

Me: Remember, you are watching a movie. You are safe.

Kim: The Yanks are surrounding the church. I smell smoke. I can hardly breathe. Sully, come back. Don't go out there. Sully, come back! I can see him running. It's too late. They shot Sully. God, help me. They shot the boy. They keep shooting him. The smoke is so bad, the heat from the fire—I am going to have to run for it. I took a last look out the window. I am trying to see where the soldiers are. I have to go now. I start running, never got fifty feet. I have been hit, and it's like fire going through my body. The pain—I have collapsed. I am on the ground. The Yanks are surrounding me. They are kicking me. I am now lying on my back. One of the Yanks is putting his rifle to my head. He is saying, "Die, you grey-coat scum." The last thing I remember is a pain in my head—and then nothing.

Me: Do you remember your name?

Kim: Yes. It was Jimmy Brett.

Me: Do you remember the date?

Kim: Yes. It's September, 1864.

I suggested to Kim that he do a little homework and see if there was a town called Marianna in Florida and if any of these memories could be proven.

After the regression, Kim immediately felt better. It was truly amazing. Kim said he felt light, upbeat. He had never realized all the guilt he was carrying—especially about fifteen-year-old Sully, who had been killed. Kim said that he had felt totally responsible for the boy's death. Kim knows now that there was nothing he could have done to save him.

Kim said, "I guess that's why I feel so comfortable living in the south. I used to hate the North, and I never knew why."

Sometime later, Kim contacted me to let me know that there was a town called Marianna. There had been a battle there during the Civil War, and to his surprise, a soldier named James Brett had been killed during that battle.

Well, needless to say, this regression shows what the experience is all about. You will not have a regression like Kim's every time. As a matter of fact, regressions like this are rare. But when you get one, it's like winning the lottery.

Winter Coats

In this case, the wife contacted me, and her name was Sandra.

Sandra went on to tell me that all her husband did was collect winter coats and boots. Their garage had been turned into a storage unit for all these winter coats. (By the way, they lived in Florida.) She didn't know where his idea for collecting winter clothes had come from. Her husband, Jim, had never been out of the state of Florida, and he refused to go anywhere where it might be cold. This really upset Sandra, because she would have loved to travel, especially to Colorado to see those snowcapped mountains.

Sandra finally convinced Jim to come and see me. She warned me that Jim thought past-life regression was a big joke and warned me to be ready.

You know, I really like it when people question everything, because when this type of people have past memories, it's like watching a child open his presents on Christmas morning—excitement without question. It absolutely changes their lives in that moment.

The following is the record of Jim's regression.

Me: Five, four, three, two, one. You are now in lifetime that you have lived before. Mentally look out through your eyes and listen with your ears. Mentally look down at your feet. What are you wearing on your feet?

Jim: It looks like an animal of some kind is on my feet. Wait, they are some sort of fur boots.

Me: Where are you?

Jim: I am in the woods, trapping and collecting furs to sell to the trading post.

Me: Do you know what year it is?

Jim: It's 1837.

Me: Describe your surroundings.

Jim: Well, today is a bright and sunny day. The ground is covered with a light snow, and I can see Rocky Mountain peaks in the distance. It feels so warm that I came out to set my trapline.

Me: Are you married?

Jim: Sad to say, I lost my wife and son during childbirth. I now live alone in my cabin. (Note: I deliberately did not question Jim about the deaths of his wife and baby. If he had wanted to talk more about it, his mind would have offered that information.)

Me: Tell me about your cabin.

Jim: I built it myself with the help of my wife, Mary. That's when we had some big disagreements. Most of the disagreements were about where to locate our cabin. It was important for me to make sure that we never got flooded after winter or rainstorms, so I wanted the cabin to be built on a higher part of the land. Mary wanted the cabin moved to where she could get the most sunlight. Eventually, we worked it out. We were lucky, because our land had some very old trees. The old trees didn't have a lot of limbs, which would have created knots in the wood. The trees were long and straight. We didn't have to do a lot of notching to make them fit. Mary would go around and fit in all the joints with bits of rocks, sticks, and mud. We had to keep the drafts out in winter. The hardest part of building the cabin was moving those big rocks to lay the logs on. It almost killed my horse and me.

Me: Tell me about yourself.

Jim: Well, I hunt for beaver fur most of the time. I am a free trapper.

Me: What is a free trapper?

Jim: Most trappers work for a company. They pretty much work to pay back for the supplies they receive. I am a free trapper, so I can sell my furs to the highest bidder. But beaver trapping is almost over.

Me: What do you mean, "almost over"?

Jim: There are so many trappers, it's become very difficult to find beaver. Now the companies are not paying very much anymore for our furs. It's the Hudson Bay Company's fault.

Me: How's is it the Hudson Bays Company's fault.

Jim: They put most of the American fur companies out of business, because they sell us our supplies for a lot cheaper than the American companies, so we all take our furs to them. Oh, no!

Me: What is it?

Jim: It's starting to snow really heavy. I came out without my coat and supplies because it was sunny and warm. I can't see anything. The snow is blinding, and I am getting very cold.

Me: What's happening now?

Jim: I am lost. I don't know my way back to the cabin. I can only see a foot in front of my face. I am getting very cold, and it's getting dark.

Me: Remember, you are here with me, safe. Just think of this as watching a movie. If you choose to open your eyes and end your regression, you can do so at any time.

Jim: I am getting very tired, cold, and hungry. I have to sit down. Every part of my body is frozen. I can't feel any part of my body. I am so sleepy, I barely can keep my eyes open.

Me: Where are you now?

Jim: I don't know, but it is very peaceful. I am not cold anymore.

Me: What was the last thing you remember?

Jim: I remember saying to myself, "I will never forget my coat and gear again."

Jim opened his eyes and ended his regression. He said he felt great and refreshed.

Then I said to Jim, "So now we know why you collect winter clothing." Jim started to laugh and said, "Yes. Now I know why."

About six months later, Jim's wife called and said that Jim had been giving his winter clothing away. It's very satisfying when you can help people like Jim.

You come across this type of regression on a regular basis. When a person has some sort of obsession, it's amazing that the mind will usually take you directly to the lifetime where the issue was created.

All you have to do is keep everything calm and ask open-ended questions. Follow the lead of your client, and he will lead you right to the problem.

CHAPTER 18

Past-Life and Age Regression Facilitator Standards for Certification

Certification from this course is granted when you provide evidence of being prepared to conduct past-life and age regressions.
The following is required to become certified:

Complete the exam below and provide a minimum of four taped past-life and/or age regressions. The tapes must be comprehensible. Forward these tapes, along with your exam and a check for $149.00 to cover the costs of the examination, to the address at the end of the exam. Once we receive the tapes, our team will review them to determine whether you meet the standards for certification.

If you meet the standards, you will receive a Certificate of Completion for the course, which states that you have met all the requirements and can now call yourself a past-life regression facilitator. You may e-mail us at any time with your questions or suggestions. We are also interested in any regressions you have conducted, where you were able to verify the information provided by the subject.

You will join an elite group of individuals who emphasize spiritual, mental, and emotional maturity and devotion to a lifestyle of service to others.

EXAMINATION FOR CERTIFICATION AS PAST-LIFE AND AGE REGRESSION FACILITATOR

Name: _____

Address: _____

Date: _____

Please note that illegible examination papers will not be graded.

1. Define *reincarnation*.

_____

_____

_____

2. Why do we reincarnate?

_____

_____

_____

3. Describe *Karma*.

_____

_____

_____

4. Define *spontaneous regression.*

_____

_____

_____

5. Define in detail *multi-level awareness.*

_____

_____

_____

6. What is the importance of the therapeutic process of regression?

_____

_____

_____

7. Explain the use of regression as a preventive therapy.

_____

_____

_____

8. What are the two rules used in determining the physical fitness of a regression subject?

_____

_____

_____

9. Name the three reasons why reincarnation was declared to be heresy.

_____

_____

_____

10. Why is record-keeping important in reincarnation research?

_____

_____

_____

11. Name and describe the six initial questions used in a regression.

_____

_____

_____

12. How is *death* defined in this course?

_____

_____

_____

13. In detail, define the *blueprint for life.*

_____

_____

_____

14. How can you tell a reincarnation dream from any other dream?

_____

_____

_____

15. How do you end recurring dreams?

_____

_____

_____

16. What is the first phase in preparing a subject for a regression?

_____

_____

_____

17. What is the process used by the facilitator to terminate a regression?

_____

_____

_____

18. What aspect immediately follows the relaxation phase?

_____

_____

_____

19. How does imagination work with regression techniques?

_____

_____

_____

20. Define *running*.

_____

_____

_____

21. Describe the problem of avoidance. What action is taken to solve the problem?

_____

_____

_____

22. Define *life scripts*.

_____

_____

_____

23. Define the problem of panic attacks. What action is taken to solve the problem?

_____

_____

_____

24. Define *recurring positive and negative patterns.*

_____

_____

_____

25. What role does suicide play in reincarnation?

_____

_____

_____

26. Define in detail what we mean by *age regression.*

_____

_____

_____

27. What kind of rabbi was Jesus?

_____

_____

_____

28. What belief did the original founders of Christianity teach about death?

_____

_____

_____

29. Name the two different times in history where reincarnation was removed from the original teachings of Christ.

_____

_____

_____

30. Why did Jesus dislike organized religion?

_____

_____

_____

31. In your opinion, why was Jesus crucified?

_____

_____

_____

32. Who crucified Jesus?

_____

_____

_____

This is the end of the exam.
Forward your exam materials along with your recordings to:

Douglas Casimiri
1324 Seven Springs Blvd. #145
New Port Richey, Florida 34655
727-277-9056
E-mail: pastlifememories@aol.com
(Please note that the recordings will not be returned.)

REFERENCES

Bean, James. *Lost Books of the Bible.* 1997 Maine Well-Being Press.

Blyth, Henry. *The Three Lives of Naomi.* 1956. Frederick Mulle, Ltd.

Clement of Alexandria. (c.150-c.211) Greek speaking thinker of the early church.

Holland John. *Power of the Soul.* 2007 Hay House, Carlsbad, California.

Dead Sea Scrolls discovered 1947, after hidden for 2,000 years.

Titus Flavius Josephus. (37-c100) Roman – Jewish Historian.

Gnostic Scrolls discovered 1945 after hidden for 2,000 years.

Hefele, Charles Joseph.(1809-1893) *A History of the Christian Councils.*

Howe, Quincy. *Reincarnation for the Christian.* 1987 A Quest Book.

Klein. *The Effects of Suggestion on Past Lives.* 1982 Baker.

Martin, Roy. *Reincarnation and Beyond.* 1942.

McClain, Florence. *Past-Life Regression.* 1997 Llewellyn Publications, St. Paul, Minnesota.

Moore, Thomas. *Soul Mates.* 1994 HarperCollins Publishers, New York, NY.

Origen (AD 185–254) Early Christian Theologian.

Potinus. Philosopher (204-270c.e.) *The Descent of the Soul.*

Puryear, Herbert Bruce. *Why Jesus Taught Reincarnation.* (1993).

Rose, Neil. *The Bishop of Nyssa, Past-Life Stories.*

The Old Testament.

The New Testament.

Cannon Alexander. *The Power of Karma in Relation to Destiny* (1936).

Howe Linda. *The Akashic Records, Sounds True, Inc2009. Boulder, Co.*

The College of Metaphysical Studies, Clearwater Florida.

ABOUT THE AUTHOR

Douglas Casimiri was born in Toronto, Canada, and now lives in Tampa, Florida.

Douglas is an international black-belt karate instructor.

A past-life regression facilitator.

Certified in the science of complementary healing.

Intuitive reader.

Printed in Great Britain
by Amazon

24692852R00098